£12.95

UNMANNED DRONE

× Architecture and Security Series ×

UNMANNED DRONE

× Ethel Baraona, Marina Otero & Malkit Shoshan (eds.) ×

CONTENTS

INTRODUCTION

9
About Unmanned. Architecture and Security Series

11
About Drone

12
Spaces of Exception
Marina Otero Verzier

READER

17
A Century of War: From the Trench to the Living Space
Malkit Shoshan

29
Creatures of the Air, Some New Occult Problems
Matthew Stadler

37
Armed Drones and International Law
Catherine Harwood

44
Twenty-first Century Birdwatching
Ruben Pater

52
Decolonized Skies: Art, the View from above and the Formation of New Civil Knowledge
Yael Messer, Gilad Reich

64
Life of a Drone Pilot
Francesca Recchia

DISCUSSION

71
Landscapes of Secrecy: Data and Reporting in the Drone Debate

73
Infrastructures of Secrecy and Public Knowledge
Dan Gettinger, Arthur Holland Mitchel

75
Landscapes of Secrecy: Discussion

101
The Drone Salon

102
A New View From Above, a Report on the Drone Salon
Jane Szita

CONCLUSION

125
From the Other Side of the Screen
Ethel Baraona Pohl

134
Contributors

Introduction

About Unmanned. Architecture and Security Series

In the last decades, the overflow of war-related innovation into the civic space has become ubiquitous, raising a global debate on the need for an enhanced state security apparatus.

The dependence on Internet communication technologies renders a large part of the world's population as both targets and active participants in a global mass surveillance infrastructure of social networks, digital displays, environmental sensors, smartphones, control rooms and drone pilot screens, to name a few. Within a constant flow of data unleashed by a pressing need to inform and be informed, the distinction between those who have the capacity to see and those who are seen is no longer self-evident.

New independent journalistic platforms emerge as rapidly as new modes of censorship and systems of web monitoring, while technologies that were once labeled as socio-political liberators have proven to be the exact opposite: the misuse of information can—and often does—contribute to the commodification of our lives and threaten our individual rights. Despite the large number of debates, articles and projects concerned with the militarization of cities, as well as the proliferation of security governance technologies, it is precisely now, more than ever, that the discussion must continue.

At the core of the *Unmanned: Architecture and Security* research and publication series is a critical analysis of the many ways in which current security affairs transform the built environment: drone technologies adopted by corporations to deliver books; embassies transformed into residences for political asylum seekers; surveillance cameras following our Sunday strolls.

In this context, *Unmanned* examines architecture's role in the construction of the contemporary security apparatus and its global spaces of exception, from detention camps to embassies, from Faraday shields to smart cities. The series brings together scholars and professionals from diverse disciplinary backgrounds—including architects, artists, human rights experts, military officials, policy-makers, hackers, and novelists—to investigate shifting notions of privacy, safety, and their spatial manifestations; to discuss the consequences of the civilian appropriation of military technologies; and to set an agenda for design professionals to engage on a technological, cultural, and political level through the exploration of three main topics —*Drone, Retreat, and Missions.*

About Drone

Drones are unmanned aircrafts. They are either remotely controlled or, increasingly, autonomously following a pre-programmed mission; they can fly solo missions or operate in formation. While initially developed for use in conflict situations, drone technologies–now faster, smaller and cheaper to produce–have permeated the civic realm and been appropriated as a tool for a variety of purposes, from filming wedding ceremonies to monitoring agricultural fields. Drones transport bombs, but also books and pizza boxes; they can be used for targeting and killing individuals, but also to provide medical assistance.

This expansion of the operational space of drone technologies is strongly connected to the possibilities offered by virtual technologies and the management of data, by which increasingly decisions are not based on conclusive evidence but on speculative scenarios. This publication aims to unpack the spatial order conveyed by drones together with its corresponding narratives, geographies and architectures.

Unmanned: Drone results from research carried out by Malkit Shoshan, Marina Otero Verzier and Ethel Baraona Pohl for two different seminars that took place in 2014. The first, *Landscapes of Secrecy*, was a panel discussion at Studio-X NYC in collaboration with the Center for the Study of the Drone; the second, the *Drone Salon*, was part of the *Drones and Honeycombs* program hosted by Rotterdam's Het Nieuwe Instituut, and provided an overview of the challenges and opportunities of fast-developing drone technologies in the battlefield and in the civic realm.

— *Ethel Baraona Pohl, Marina Otero Verzier, Malkit Shoshan*

UNMANNED   ARCHITECTURE AND SECURITY SERIES

Spaces of Exception
Marina Otero Verzier

Unmanned Aerial Vehicles (UAVs) have become a central tool of the U.S. national security strategy, encapsulating the whole narrative of the "war on terror" and its unbounded global armed conflict. Founded on the rhetoric of the lawlessness, remoteness and insecurity of the territories of terrorist hideouts, the drone program allows the U.S. to conduct covert strikes in countries such as Pakistan, Afghanistan, Yemen or Somalia from military bases in the homeland. A remote controlled war is carried out under the cover of secrecy and in the name of security.

Above—where most of the modernist dreams of utopian architecture were situated—and detached from the ground, there is a space where normal law is suspended and emergency becomes the rule. This is the space navigated by combat drones, from where their visual feed dictates the politics of seeing, domesticating and gaining control over a *remote* land.

The drone feed provides a distant, legible image of the territory, turning it into an artifact that can be understood, controlled and subjugated according to calculated managerial principles and engineering techniques. Every piece of so-called "gathered intelligence" finds its place in a suspended terrain; an imposed matrix organized around the oversimplified notions of "military targets," "civilians" and "collateral damage."

Even if both war scenarios—the control rooms from where drones are operated and the sites of their missions—are spatially distant, the strikes make the spatio-temporal dimension of drone pilots, satellite links, targets and the different sovereignties to which they might belong converge. Along with the geopolitical transformations associated with the rise of drone strikes, the program conveys a multi-scalar, juridical and spatial order that needs to be unpacked together with its corresponding narratives, economies and architectures.

One of the ways in which this order can be theorized is through Giorgio Agamben's rumination on the state of exception.[1] As Agamben notes, in Western democracies we see an "unprecedented generalization of the paradigm of security as the normal technique of government." The result, according to Agamben, is a situation in which the very distinction between peace and war becomes impossible. This, we could claim, is the space of the drone program; a space of absolute indeterminacy between legal and illegal, war and peace, law and violence. Paradoxically, this space of legal and sovereign indeterminacy is presented and normalized by the administration as a lawful, effective and precise instrument of counter-terrorism. The drone's view is extrapolated into a template for structuring a global security regime, and its associated aesthetics and mechanisms of representation.

Social normalization manifests the political potential of representation, but representational techniques can also be leveraged as essential instruments to expose how this secret and invisible program materializes in the ground, from the sound of the drone circling in the sky to the dramatic effects of its strikes. By documenting, visualizing and reporting the spatial order constructed by the drone program, we might be able to unveil what is hidden from public view and compel government accountability. In this context, data becomes prerequisite for enhancing our capacity to see the drone warfare, from material details to large geopolitical questions; from the concealed gaze of the drone operator to the invisibility of the victims.

If Jeremy Bentham's Panopticon is, as discussed in the work of Michel Foucault, an ideal architectural model of modern disciplinary power, what, we might ask, is the spatial and legal assemblage of contemporary power constructed by drone strikes? And how it could be visualized?

UNMANNED   ARCHITECTURE AND SECURITY SERIES

These and other questions are explored in this volume, which brings together researchers from diverse disciplinary backgrounds whose work seeks to understand and represent the nature and extent of drone operations and the relationship between secrecy and forms of surveillance and violence. Once it is part of our imaginary, the powerful view of the drone virtually cancels any other understanding of reality. *Drone* seeks to revert and unpack that maneuver.

---

1   Giorgio Agamben, *State of Exception*, trans. Kevin Attell (Chicago and London: The University of Chicago Press, 2005), 14, 22

Reader

A Century of War: From the Trench to the Living Space
Malkit Shoshan

In his book *War & Peace*, Tolstoy described two type of spaces. The ballrooms, the living spaces of the people, and the battlefields, the far away militarized zone where the battle was fought. This dichotomy is no longer there.

The View from Above, 2014–1914

Modernity first manifested itself at a grand scale during the First World War. A hundred years later, some developments such as drone warfare and the ever-expanding battlefield, can be traced back to the early decades of the twentieth century. By looking at these big issues and understanding their development with a century of historical perspective, we can become better equipped in dealing with future challenges.

In 1914, aviation became the ultimate way of seeing. Flying allowed the production of an uninterrupted stream of images; millions of negatives were produced, capturing daily the conditions on enemy ground. It was the first military industrial conflict.

The occupation of airspace was primarily a conquest of space for the sake of seeing. At the core of this practice was a mechanism of distant and covert inspection that allowed the application of military supremacy over another territory.

During these years, vertical perspective and a view of the world from above emerged with the introduction of zeppelins and airplanes. Aerial photograph documented large areas of land, the battlefield, cities and landscapes. The combination of the ability to fly and see the ground from above became a fundamental instrument of modern warfare and spatial planning, changing the way we perceive and relate to our living environment. It liberated the thought and the imagination from the limitation of the horizontal view.

The representation of the view from above—the aerial photograph—led to the invention of tools for its analysis, codification and transformation into visual information, in the form of detailed maps and plans of different scales, among others. These devices changed not only the battlefield but the approach towards urban design, such as with the relationship between the city and the countryside. They helped to relate territories and programs to one another—connecting, overlapping or separating them, and making the distance between elements in space increasingly smaller.

The conquest of vertical space that started in the First World War continues today with the use of drones. Airplanes changed the way we see the world; drones change the way we see, feel and interact with our surroundings. The intuitive movement of the drone, its sensors and the way it can be controlled from afar allow us to see things not just from above but from all directions—vertically, horizontally, and any angle in between. We can see heat prints and sounds, both inside and outside. The analytical capacity of the machines can read not just objects and movements in space, but also recognize social connections and relationships between one person and another, rendering the information that is captured from above progressively more articulated and detailed.

The drone and its technology accelerate the scientific processes that came into view with the period of the First World War. The battlefield has moved from the trench into the civic space. Cities, villages and homes are the primary objects in the contemporary theater of war.

The War and the City

In 2006, General David H. Petraeus published a cutting-edge manual titled *Counterinsurgency (FM 3-24 / MCWP 3-33.5)* In this volume, Petraeus, who led the NATO forces in Iraq and

A CENTURY OF WAR

The Trench no.1. An impression of '2014-1914. The view from above' exhibition by Malkit Shoshan. Het Nieuwe Instituut. March 2014

UNMANNED ARCHITECTURE AND SECURITY SERIES

The Trench no.2. An impression of '2014-1914. The view from above' exhibition by Malkit Shoshan. Het Nieuwe Instituut. March 2014

The Trench no.3. An impression of '2014-1914. The view from above' exhibition by Malkit Shoshan. Het Nieuwe Instituut. March 2014

A CENTURY OF WAR

The Trench and The Drone. An impression of '2014-1914. The view from above' exhibition by Malkit Shoshan. Het Nieuwe Instituut. March 2014

UNMANNED ARCHITECTURE AND SECURITY SERIES

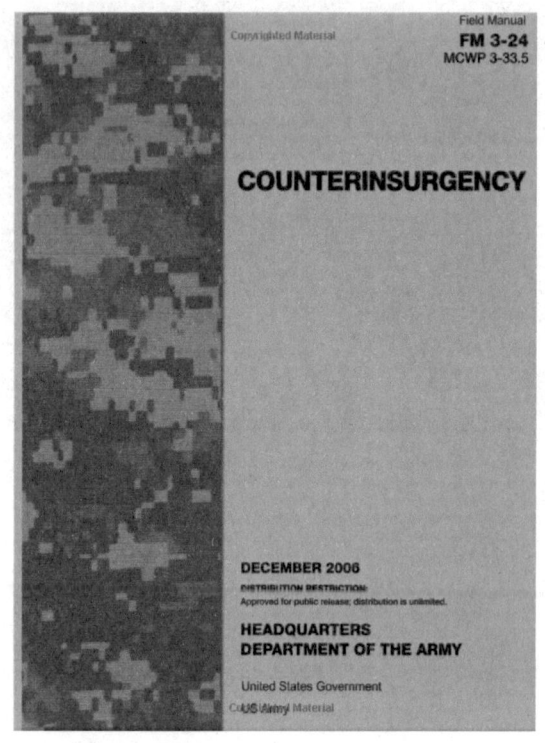

The Counterinsurgency Manual (U.S. Gov. 2006)

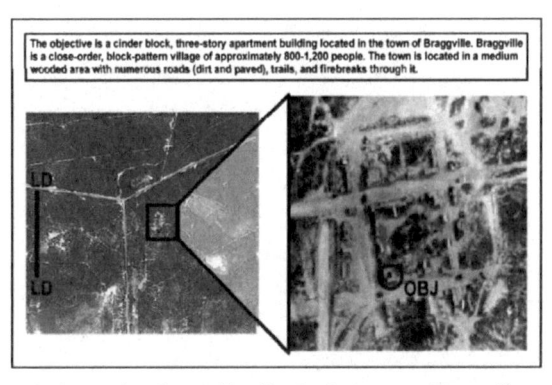

> The objective is a cinder block, three-story apartment building located in the town of Braggville. Braggville is a close-order, block-pattern village of approximately 800-1,200 people. The town is located in a medium wooded area with numerous roads (dirt and paved), trails, and firebreaks through it.

An impression of target identification in the town of Braggville.
Counterinsurgency Manual (U.S. Gov. 2006)

Afghanistan, introduced the "Small Wars Doctrine," in which warfare takes place within inhabited areas.

The general was notorious for his interest in the civic realm, leaving behind the era of wars between national armies battling for territorial supremacy: for Petraeus, the main theater of war was the city. For him the soldier should not be only a warrior, but also a school teacher and a nurse,[2] his actions fully inserted in daily civic life. The scope of Petraeus' concept was to radically re-think the civic realm; he tailored counterinsurgency (coin) warfare[3] to the contemporary conditions in the city. The *Counterinsurgency Manual* describes the battlefield as a succession of small, inhabited enclaves with all kinds of security hazards applied to a day-to-day civic environment; soldiers are taught to clear thesespaces from threat, and once eliminated, to rebuild them anew through an intense process of reconstruction and disciplinary training of the local population[4]. Eventually, Petraeus' doctrine was formalized into four main methodological phases: Shape, Clear, Hold and Build.

In the first phase, Shape, the environment is studied. To identify a threat, soldiers need to understand the logic of the civic space, the way it is built, organized and used by its inhabitants. They need to observe homes, neighborhoods, villages and cities,

UNMANNED   ARCHITECTURE AND SECURITY SERIES

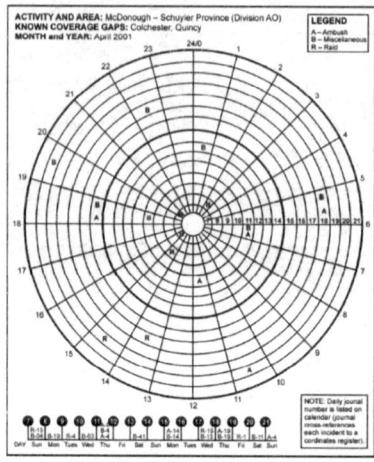

Figure B-14. Example pattern analysis plot sheet

Threat identification in the civic space based on behavioral and movement patterns. Counterinsurgency Manual (U.S. Gov. 2006)

Social Network Analysis diagrams
Interaction between people in a civic environment

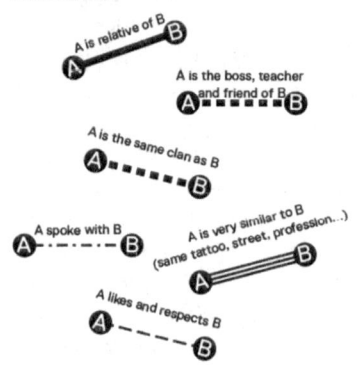

Threat identification based on social relations and networks.
Counterinsurgency Manual (U.S. Gov. 2006)

document how people move in space and interact with one another on social, cultural and financial levels.

Information collected during the Shape phase turns into a long list of action possibilities that link together people, places, networks, and behavioral rituals. Civic, personal and communal activities are classified, codified and turned into data, assembling a threat matrix that could highlight abnormality and insurgent activities.

In Iraq and Afghanistan, soldiers were allowed to conduct disruption operations in people's living environments in order to weaken insurgents' ability to control an area; similarly, they were allowed to carry out operations to force insurgents to alter their course of action, enriching the database of action, reaction and probability of abnormality. These wars proved that combat in an urban space is perpetual, complicated, costly and messy. Consequently, an alternative had to be found.

COIN by a Drone

Drones are unmanned aircraft, controlled from afar, or autonomously following a pre-set mission. Equipped with sensors, they are able to provide detailed views of selected environments.

Their sensors can render pictures of reality in real time, capturing indoor and outdoor views, tracing the movements of individuals in space even days after they take place. Ultimately, drones can identify social, economic and cultural networks, allowing the former human observation phase, Shape, to be performed from afar.

In this way, the proof-based identification of threat turns into the disposition matrix,[5] an algorithm-based automated system that highlights the probability of future abnormality.

The transformation of wars between nations into a new form of warfare between global coalitions and insurgents didn't result only in the invasion of remote landscapes—in countries like Iraq and Afghanistan—by military and surveillance technologies. The search for insurgents and counterinsurgency methods spilled over the epicenter of war, with similar techniques of data collec-

UNMANNED ARCHITECTURE AND SECURITY SERIES

The space and apparatus of the drone operator.
Confessions of a Drone Warrior. Flying a drone can feel like a deadly
two-person video game—with a pilot (left) and sensor (right). [6]

tion and surveillance ubiquitously entering society, including our domestic space, to detect an immanent threat.

The Mountain of Waziristan

Wherever we are, our society is stepping into an unknown future where mass surveillance is a common practice, a world that is deconstructed according to counterinsurgency methods and where the detection of abnormality comes first. It is hard to speculate what the future will bring without falling into an Orwellian scenario.[7]

Answers to the consequence of current warfare and how it affects the civic realm might be found in the fringes of Waziristan, a province where people are being targeted daily by drones, but perhaps also in Berlin, a city known to be a safe haven for hackers seeking to escape the U.S. National Security Agency (NSA).

In 2012, the International Human Rights and Conflict Resolution Clinic at the Stanford Law School published the "Living Under Drones" report,[8] after sending researchers to examine the effect of drones in a Zaraki village in North Waziristan.

Researchers collected testimonies of inhabitants: their stories expressed a great deal of fear of everything that is ordinary.

People described their fear of the outdoors; daily activities such as grocery shopping or sending children to school were laced with a great deal of pressure. Their anxiety of others exponentially grew. Ultimately, they could never tell who is on the "target list" and who could expose them to the strike of the drone. The order of civility collapsed altogether, and people began to live in isolation.

In their accounts, however, they long for happiness, for a time when they could talk freely with one another or dream of the future. The drone, however, imposed a new state of survival that shadowed everything else.

Elsewhere in the globe, a different reality emerges. Software developer Ladar Levinson moved from the U.S. to Berlin in his attempt to escape the NSA. Out of moral conscience, Levinson refused to share the database of his software users with the NSA, becoming one of the most prominent voices against mass surveillance and violation of privacy. In 2013, he addressed the EU parliament in order to explain the NSA's extensive surveillance devices:

> "What we have here today is a debate on to what length a government and its law enforcement officers should be allowed to go when it comes to conducting investigations. It's the simple question of 'surveillance versus privacy' and a lot of people have accused me of being anti-government because I was anti-surveillance and that's simply not true—I'm not anti-government, I'm simply pro-freedom. Think about that. I believe in the rule of law; I believe in the need to conduct investigations. But those investigations are supposed to be difficult for a reason. It is meant to be difficult to invade somebody's privacy because of how intrusive it is. Because of how disruptive it is. If we don't have a right to privacy how do we have a free and open discussion? What good is the right to free speech if it's not protected, in the sense that you can have a private discussion with somebody else about something you disagree with? Think about the chilling effect that has on countries that don't have a right to privacy. It's one thing for

us to give up our rights for what we guaranteed is the ability to talk about the rights that we've lost in the hope."[9]

The zeppelins first liberated us from the horizontal view and gave us a new perspective of the city and the world. A century later, the evolution of First World War technologies has transformed them into the primary threat to our freedom, rapidly penetrating every aspect of our living world, our cities, our homes and our relationships with one another.

This essay is based on the activities and presentations held around the author's research project Drones and Honeycombs, which have materialized in occasions such as the "Drone Salon" seminar and the exhibition "2014-1914, The view from above," at Het Nieuwe Instituut, Rotterdam.

1   Tolstoy, Leo. *War and Peace*; Macmillan, 1942.
2   Muggah, Robert *Stabilization Operations, Security and Development: States of Fragility* (Routledge, 2014).
3   Nagl, John A. *Counterinsurgency Lessons from Malaya and Vietnam: Learning to Eat Soup with a Knife* (Praeger, 2002).
4   Brendan Mcquade. "The Return of Domestic CounterInsurgency?" *Counter Punch*, April 29, 2011, accessed May 24, 2016, http://www.counterpunch.org/2011/04/29/the-return-of-domestic-counterinsurgency/
5   Ian Cobain. "Obama's secret kill list — the disposition matrix", *The Guardian*, July 14, 2013, accessed May 24, 2016, http://www.theguardian.com/world/2013/jul/14/obama-secret-kill-list-disposition-matrix
6   Levitas, Ethan, and Power, Matthew. "Confessions of an American Drone Operator." GQ, 22 Oct. 2013, www.gq.com/story/drone-uav-pilot-assassination
7   "If you want to keep a secret, you must also hide it from yourself." George Orwell, *1984* (Harvill Secker, 1949).
8   Cavallaro, James, and Stephan Sonnenberg. "Living under Drones: Death, Injury, and Trauma to Civilians" from *U.S. Drone Practices in Pakistan* (Stanford Law School, 2012).
9   "Meeting 'Privacy Platform, Surveillance vs. Encryption. Who's Winning the Cat and Mouse Game?'", European Parliament Audiovisual Services for Media, October 15, 2013, accessed May 24, 2016, http://audiovisual.europarl.europa.eu/Assetdetail.aspx?id=98fc5d27-c1e9-442e-91f3-a25800ddf384

Creatures of the Air, Some New Occult Problems
Matthew Stadler

"Just before evening, two sentries saw a dark cloud flying toward them in a clear sky and thought they could hear the voices of many people jumbled together inside it, although neither man actually saw anyone. The one sentry, more daring than the other, said 'What is all this? Do you think we're safe? If you like, I'll aim my gun at that cloud.' His companion agreed. He shot, there was a thunderclap and a woman fell down from the cloud at their feet. She was drunk, naked, very fat, middle-aged, and her thigh had been shot through twice. They arrested her, but she began to pretend she was deranged and said scarcely anything in reply to their questions."[1]

The year is 1584. We are in Saxon Germany. This woman, the sentries know, is a witch. Her marriage to Satan and the dry, rough sexual intercourse she had with Him, has given her deadly powers that she visits on innocent people and animals, flying invisibly or in darkness, often in large swarms, accompanied by other maleficent creatures of the air, to deliver her fatal charms without being seen. She is the flash point of terror for a whole continent: Europe in the sixteenth century.

Sixteenth-century Europe abounded with terrifying airborne powers: invisible forces of black magic that were disturbingly like the positive forces of white magic, the angels and spirits of the church, that protected the faithful and promised them the glory of heaven when they died. Marking and navigating the boundary between black magic and white magic was the most urgent task facing that time's creative industries—artists, writers, theologians, demonologists and philosophers. What we call occult philosophy was one of the toolkits they made for navigating this treacherous and urgent problem.

Today, we face similar occult problems, but we haven't recognized them as such. Occult knowledge is knowledge of what is hidden. Occult problems are as pressing in the twenty-first century as they were in the sixteenth; yet we act as though there is no history to the problems we face. Dazzled by the newness of technologies, the problem's long ancestry is overlooked. In drones and digital networks we face the world of Hieronymus Bosch, Pieter Bruegel, Albrecht Dürer, Paracelsus, John Dee and Heinrich Cornelius Agrippa, and we should enlist their help.

How did such distinct, distant times turn up such similar problems? What sixteenth-century conditions are coming to the fore, again, in the twenty-first century? Primarily, we live amidst a rupture in the stability of the real, and a corollary rupture in the stability of the self, the subjective observer.

We credit certain modes of representation as "real," for instance a photograph. Obviously, we know the difference between a photo and what's actually there. But the photo, in this example, is credited with conveying "objective" truth, that is, the status of things independent of our subjective looking. We locate our own subjectivity in relation to it, the particular tint or distortions we add to the visible. Every mode of representation is a systematic distortion of one kind or another, but we credit a particular system of distortion with the virtue of "realism," so that we can calculate, measure, or know our subjective position using the real as our benchmark.

So, for example, photography. A photograph shows reality, and deviations from it—anything at odds with the camera's record—become evidence of subjectivity, showing the witness's bias, say, or the painter's "impressions." In earlier times, perspective drawing emerged as a similarly powerful technology, claiming a kind of realism that refigured other modes of representation, other accounts—flat iconic religious painting, for example—as either subjective or mystical, and in any event, unrealistic. When the real is destabilized, a corollary disruption blurs or dissolves the stability of the subject, the "I" who stands in relation to what is "real," in the same way that the washing away of land changes the shape of the sea.

The sixteenth century shares with our time a remarkable rupture in the regime of realism. In the sixteenth century, the emergence of perspectival technology and then a related optical fidelity in drawing—displayed in Dürer's drawings of animals, portraits of people, and so on—disrupted the authority of iconic religious painting. In the twenty-first century, digital manipulation of photographic imagery has disrupted the authority of the camera. The two are sort of flip-side, reverse disruptions. In the earlier instance, a human-centered, optical realism—the authority of the human eye—rose to displace the authority of religious, iconic images. Today, the same human-centered optical regime—enacted using cameras—is being eroded by a numerological, mystical system: the programmer's mathematical manipulations of digital information.

The intervening five hundred years of stability might be called the regime of the eye. This period has also been called Humanism; and the defenders of Humanism are worried that the clarity of human authority is now dissolved in a tide of cyborgs and inter-species collaboration. Before, under Humanism's reign, representation was considered accurate and truthful however closely it mimicked human optical experience—the operations of binaural vision. The regime of the eye dawned with perspectival technologies and optical fidelity in drawing. And now it is setting, as the stability of the photograph or video is undone in a rising tide of digital manipulations and digitally generated visual representations. We're now able to create completely immersive, navigable visual fields never ever using optical devices—only digits shaping pixels on a screen. We descend again into numerology.

During both ruptures—in the sixteenth-century rise of the regime of the eye; and now, amidst its decline—the stable subject, the person, became destabilized as realism liquefied around us, leaking into and out of the authoring subject. What is "real"—i.e., stable outside of us—and what is our doing? In times of rupture and change we cannot know. Drones—especially digitally networked drones—destabilize the regime of the eye more profoundly than other technological developments of our time. Their profound undermining effect is beautifully displayed in the fairly recent development of the "drone selfie."

When aircraft were manned, a pilot flew a plane into the air and he became a threat to his enemies below. You've seen the iconic image, an armed man in an airplane, looking down, readying his bomb. Or, from the opposite point of view, frightened civilians looking worriedly up from their ruins at a speck in the sky. But the unmanned aircraft has no man. It is piloted, typically, by a soldier in a windowless room. He guides it through a shifting matrix of digital coordinates, revealed on his computer screen and correlated to a video image from an onboard camera. It is possible that his enemies, the ones charged with neutralizing the threat of the drone, also sit in windowless rooms watching digital information stream by. Such language as "lifting off," "dropping" bombs, and "above" or "below" are archaic residues from the old experience of airborne pilots. They serve a kind of metaphorical function for a seated man tracking the flow of digital information indoors. The numbers tell him, and the video image confirms, that the drone has drawn near its target, taken a bead, and then struck —completing the mission before disappearing again, perhaps never ever having been seen.

Whose drone is it? Where is the threat? When we become targets, of what are we the target? Where, in this matrix of threat—through which the drone as a remote instrument moves —is the enemy, the malevolence? And where are we in relation to it? If the drone is an instrument of our own government, are we both the target and the aggressor? Subject/object relations are scrambled. We are caught in occult problems. In a "drone selfie," where is the self?

CREATURES OF THE AIR

Similarly—if the individual can be spread across this distance by the integrated system of the remote control drone—what about so-called "Unmanned Aerial Vehicles" whose operation is tethered to political and organizational tools that disperse agency across entire populations? Connect drones to technologies such as military decision-making software, such as the so-called "democratic elections" and "representative government," and we find whole populations similarly stretched—their status as subject or object of, say, drone strikes, hopelessly scrambled. As with the eager shutterbug and his drone-selfie, the democratic citizen is bombing himself whenever Obama orders a drone-strike against a U.S. citizen. If there is such a thing as a global citizen, in the feedback loop of democratic process, we are all bombing ourselves constantly.

But of course we aren't global citizens and there are no real democracies. Readers of this text, for example, cannot stop Obama's drone strikes. But what about "likes" on Facebook? Or crowdfunding? Or Eurovision Song Contests? If we have agency in densely interconnected networks, how can we locate or delineate the self and what lies outside? However imperfectly, digitization aspires to disperse agency across a blurred field of subjects.

We hear the words "white magic" and "black magic," "alchemy," "witches," or "angels," and we often think the discussion has strayed far from the pragmatic realm of *Realpolitik* that our work ought to engage or effect. But we should recall that in the sixteenth century these words and the forces they described were at the heart of the political struggles that drove and shaped such world-changing developments as the "British Empire"—a conception, and a political strategy that emerged directly from the work and concepts of John Dee. This first form of political globalism—imperialism—was shaped by creative responses to occult problems.

In our time, then, we should not ask how magic or alchemy or angels, per se, can become available to us as tools or concepts. We should ask what language we use today for the forces these words described in earlier times. They are still at work in the world. And they are still at the heart of political struggle. It's useful to recall the great crisis in sixteenth-century magic was how nearly identical black magic, and the demons it released, appeared in relation to white magic, with its appeal to angels and "good" Christian forces.

So, in our time, what language do we give to split the hair between legitimate power and illegitimate power? One example is the difference between "state" violence and "terrorist" violence. The two manifest almost identically, but "state" violence carries the mantle of public will—as though the putatively democratic processes behind its authority turns the magic from black, the demonic Devil's work of terrorism, to white, the salvation offered by state intervention as a protection against terrorism. We routinely accept the "white magic" of deeply intrusive, violent, and de-humanizing state activities to protect us from so-called "terrorists." This is clearly an occult problem.

What are some of the similarities between then and now? The mirror images presented between white magic and black magic are echoed in the contemporary pair of anti-terrorism and terrorism. The use of torture to elicit confessions. The need of interrogators to provide the story for the confessor to deliver. The active role played by anti-terrorists (the CIA and FBI in the U.S.) cultivating, staffing, supplying, and carrying out terrorism (to catch those "likely" to be terrorists). The baffling hall of mirrors within which anti-terrorists try to maintain their identity as separate from—and more virtuous than—terrorists. The demographic biases of the division—the poor and foreign are terrorists; the rich and native, not—, echoing the bias in the witch craze—witches are single women, usually older, often poor or common. The impossibility of any disinterested position: to not be vigilant against terrorism is to encourage it; to criticize or question anti-terrorism aids and abets terrorists.

Our new occult problems are the product of deep contradiction within enlightenment philosophies, contradictions that are only becoming intractable as philosophy achieves a kind of extremity of expression and refinement that hitherto was not possible. Ironically, what is hidden stands in plain sight. The drone—networked to as transparent and penetrating a system of communication as has ever been known—is the most complete articulation of this contradiction.

I don't aim to establish that this or that technology as good or evil. I'm trying to acknowledge familiar problems—our old friend, the subject-object crisis—and benefit by recalling what happened the last time we dealt with them. What went well or poorly in the sixteenth century, when profound ruptures in a previously stable regime of the real led to new ideas about the forces that, invisibly, filled the air? Burning witches—good idea, or bad? Or the ritual destruction of church icons? How about the institutionalization of new regimes? When the aspirations of hermetic, occult philosophers, such as Isaac Newton—his "gravity" is itself an occult notion, a hidden force—became refigured as "Enlightenment science," soon followed the founding of the Royal Society; the curriculum of the natural sciences; the displacement of mystical authority with empirical, observer-based authority. Do we face similar institutional changes? And, if so, should we aid or resist them?

It is more disturbing to hear a threat without seeing it, than to see a threat that is silent. The most common example, well known to us from camp-outs, is the mosquito. We all know the intense discomfort of hearing the mosquito's thin whine suddenly grow louder, darting near our ears, unseen. It is so aggravating that we swat at our own heads and box our ears trying to kill it. When an unseen threat can kill you, not just annoy you, the sound of its approach becomes truly terrifying. So it is with drones. Drone operators report a repeated action in their targets, on hearing the drone's whine grow louder or the roar of its missile launch arrive well ahead of the missile itself—a sudden panicked crouch and then the darting they call "scatter." Scatter is as pointless and as self-defeating a maneuver as are the hard slaps we deliver to our heads chasing mosquitoes. And it is the last act of many drone strike victims.

Faced with drones, we are still swatting at our own heads, rather than boldly stepping into alliance with Bosch and Bruegel. Where is our equivalent to Bruegel's *The Fall of the Rebel Angels*? Where is our shared intelligence about the occult? Faced with occult problems, we must not hesitate to cultivate our occult powers.

How is that done? How does one pursue "knowledge of what is hidden?" To begin, we develop the skill of looking for the hidden, rather than looking for what is there. This is difficult in a culture still dominated by Enlightenment values: the hidden is suspect; shadows only hide perils; whatever is useful has been thrown into the bright light of day.

The odyssey of Edward Snowden illustrates this. Snowden's bold step was to decide that whatever was hidden offered a key to the reality we were all living. Rather than accept the division his employers imposed—the difference between what is public and what must be kept secret—Snowden collected all the secrets and made them available to the public, to be inspected, described, commented on, turned into evidence or art or images of outrage. He placed hidden knowledge at the center of our shared inquiry, as would any good occult philosopher.

Is that maneuver possible in our lives? We are not NSA employees: generally, we are artists or writers or simply citizens who move through the world in a blur of foregrounded subject-matter and shadowed—"hidden" would be too strong a word—logistics that make up the cultural logic of our time. But perhaps the answers lie closer to us than we might think. We can start by looking at the past. And delve for a while in Bruegel's *The Fall of the Rebel Angels*.

---

[1] P.G. Maxwell-Stuart. *Martin del Rio. Investigations into Magic* (Manchester University Press, 2000). 197.

Armed Drones and International Law
Catherine Harwood

Armed drones, in themselves, are not prohibited weapons in international law, and in theory, existing international law is sufficient to govern their use.[1] But in practice, the use of drones has shone a spotlight onto areas of uncertainty and disagreement in international law. This contribution explores these questions in discussing how the use of armed drones interacts with international rights and protections. The use of drones is relevant to many international legal fields, including the law relating to the use of force, international humanitarian law and international human rights law. Some issues are less about uncertainty of law, and are rather issues of enforcement. It is difficult to ensure compliance with international law when the actors who hold power to enforce the rules those who also have a duty to abide by them.

Law Relating to the Use of Force

Entry into a foreign state's airspace must occur on a recognized legal basis. Unlawful use of force violates state sovereignty and may be considered an act of aggression. Unlike civil aviation, the use of armed drones is unsurprisingly not governed by a multilateral treaty regime, and evidence of state consent is not always easy to detect. Oblique evidence of consent can include allowing drones to use airfields and sharing intelligence. A state's private consent to the use of drones may nonetheless generate perceptions that its territory has been violated.

If a state has not consented, it is only lawful to use force with the permission of the Security Council or when acting in legitimate self-defense. The customary right to self-defense, recalled in article 51 of the United Nations Charter, allows a state to use force to protect itself from an armed attack. Traditionally, attacks came from other states. But there is an interesting question whether self-defense can be invoked against non-state actors located in third states. The problem is that in order to respond to the non-state actor, the state will violate another state's territorial sovereignty. It is unsettled whether this kind of attack engages the right to self-defense, but some commentators suggest that it should, provided the attack is sufficiently serious to be compared to an attack by a state. There are also strict criteria for self-defense to be lawfully exercised: use of proportionate force when there are no adequate alternative ways to ward off an attack. While there is a right to self-defense against a threat of attack, the threat must be imminent[2] and the response must be proportionate, which includes compliance with International Humanitarian Law.[3]

Protections of International Humanitarian Law

International Humanitarian Law (IHL) recognizes protections for civilians and other protected persons, such as wounded soldiers and prisoners of war. It makes allowances for the realities of armed conflict, and permits a greater degree of violence. But IHL only applies in situations recognized as either international or non-international armed conflicts. International Armed Conflicts (IACs) are between states, while Non-International Armed Conflicts (NIACs) are between a state and non-state armed groups, or among such groups.

For a situation to be a NIAC, violence must reach a certain intensity and non-state actors must have a certain level of organization.[4] The traditional model of a NIAC is a civil war. Many modern conflicts don't fit this paradigm, as non-state armed groups might be based in third states, so that the conflict goes beyond the state's borders. The intensity threshold may not be met, and groups may not be organized like traditional military structures. Attempts have been made to recognize broader battlefield boundaries through the concept of "spillover,"[5] which is most convincing when a conflict in one state spreads into a neighboring country. But how can a conflict "spill over" when the threat emanates from beyond the state's borders? Such questions invite the accusation that IHL remains "one war behind reality."

While politicians have embraced the concept of the global war on terror, the traditional categories of armed conflict remain prerequisites for the application of IHL. Two fundamental principles are distinction and proportionality. According to the principle of distinction, parties to a conflict must distinguish civilians from military objectives, and may only direct attacks against the latter. It is forbidden to direct attacks at civilians.[6] Parties must also take all feasible precautions to determine whether a person is a civilian.[7] In case of doubt, a person is presumed to be protected.[8]

In IACs, states may target the armed forces of opposing states, which have combatant status.[9] Combatants can be lawfully targeted at any time, unless they are hors de combat, for instance by being wounded or detained as prisoners of war. In NIACs, members of organized armed groups may be targeted if they have a continuous combat function.[10] Groups without a clear chain of command, such as loose terror cells, might not be sufficiently organized. In such cases, individuals are protected as civilians unless and until they directly participate in hostilities.[11] The concept of direct participation has not been defined in IHL. The International Committee of the Red Cross proposes a strict test, which includes the requirement that the act is likely to cause harm to the military operations or capacity of the opposing party.[12]

Another fundamental principle of IHL is the principle of proportionality.[13] While attacks directed against civilians are prohibited, IHL permits some collateral damage–incidental damage to civilians and civilian property. Attacks are proportionate when the expected harm to civilians and civilian objects is not excessive in relation to the anticipated concrete and direct military advantage of the attack.

Drones have been used in personality strikes and signature strikes. Personality strikes are against "high-value" targets: individuals targeted due to their identity, function and importance. A signature strike, by contrast, is based on a person's characteristics, when his or her identity is not known.[14] So-called "signatures" indicate whether a person is directly participating in hostilities. States provide little information about the types of characteristics they look for. Media outlets have reported that indicators include associating with known terrorists.[15] This is unlikely to amount to direct participation in hostilities. Media have also alleged that the U.S. administration considers "militants" as "all military-age males in a strike zone".[16] This reverses the presumption that in case of doubt, a person is a civilian, and would violate IHL. Where a drone strike is directed at military objectives, it must also be proportionate. Depending on the value of the target, high civilian casualties may mean that the attack is disproportionate.

These concerns apply to military technology used today. Drones are autonomous weapons insofar as they are controlled remotely, but human beings remain in control of targeting decisions. In the future, drones may be fully autonomous, selecting targets on their own. Doomsday predictions of a robot apocalypse might sound far-fetched, but states actively developing fully autonomous weapons include at least four of the five permanent members of the United Nations' Security Council.[17] Fully autonomous weapons give rise to critical questions as to whether human capacities to judge proportionality and distinguish civilians from combatants could–and should–be transferred to machines. Supporters of these technologies argue that human error is likely to cause more harm than decisions made by artificial technologies. "A robot cannot hate, cannot fear, cannot be hungry or tired and has no survival instinct."[18] But neither can robots empathize or show mercy. From a technical perspective, it is debatable whether robotic systems will ever be able to analyze information with the same sophistication, flexibility and speed as a human brain.

Turning from battlefield compliance to enforcement, fully autonomous weapons also have repercussions in terms of accountability. Criminal responsibility for war crimes requires a guilty mind. Autonomous weapons systems that bypass human decision-making mean that the mental element may not be satisfied. There are also problems with causal proximity. Computer programmers and manufacturers may be responsible for creating weapons that make incorrect targeting decisions, but these people are far from the battlefield. To permit robots to autonomously kill could lead to the breakdown of the framework of accountability. These near-future capabilities should be considered now, if IHL is to ever catch up with developments in military technology.

International Human Rights Law

Human Rights Law encompasses a broad range of civil, political, social, economic and cultural rights. Human rights treaties provide that states must respect the rights of individuals subject to its jurisdiction.[19] Generally, a state has human rights obligations when it has effective control over territory or when a person is within "the power or effective control" of a state.[20] Some states, however, do not accept that they owe human rights obligations abroad.[21] The International Court of Justice has ruled that human rights endure in armed conflicts.[22] Outside of armed conflict, states must act within a law enforcement paradigm, which requires legal force to be used as a matter of last resort, in accordance with the right to life.[23]

Human rights have an important procedural dimension. States must investigate serious violations of human rights and if found prosecute those responsible. Victims also have the right to obtain remedies for violations. In 2014, the Human Rights Council resolved that states must "ensure transparency" in the use of drones and ensure "prompt, independent and impartial investigations whenever there are indications of any violation to human rights" caused by drone operations.[24] It is notable that Pakistan tabled this resolution, and also interesting that opposition to the resolution came from the most prolific users of drones. From a human rights perspective, greater transparency is necessary. But it is also necessary to assess the legality of their use in the first place. Disputed figures of civilian causalities and uncertainty as to whether states have consented to drones in their territories demonstrate a lack of transparency surrounding their use. Without information, it is very difficult to determine whether their use complies with international law.

Concluding thoughts

While no new rules of international law are required to govern armed drones, their use has brought into sharp relief areas of international law that could be clarified, including the ambit of self-defense, the applicability and rules of IHL and the reach of International Human Rights law. While much of the drone debate focuses on questions of battlefield compliance, strengthening accountability for violations remains vital. States that violate international law may be held internationally responsible, as may states that knowingly assist such operations.[25] On an individual level, drone pilots and commanders may be responsible for international crimes.[26] While responsibility may attach in the abstract, ensuring accountability in concrete terms has proved to be more problematic. The first step towards effective oversight and accountability regarding armed drones is ensuring greater transparency regarding their use.

1   Advisory Committee on Issues of Public International Law, 'Advisory Report on Armed Drones', Advisory Report No. 23, 2013; S. Breau et al, and 'Drone Attacks, International Law, and the Recording of Civilian casualties of Armed Conflict', Oxford Research Group (2011).
2   A. Rendt, 'International Law and the Preemptive Use of Military Force', *The Washington Quarterly* 89 (2003) 26(2).
3   Legality of the Threat or Use of Nuclear Weapons, Advisory Opinion, *ICJ Reports* (1996), 226, para. 42.

4. Prosecutor v Tadic, Judgment, IT-94-1-T, 7 May 1997, paras. 561-568; Additional Protocol II 1977 to the Geneva Conventions 1949, art. 1.
5. R. Geiß, 'Armed violence in fragile states: Low-intensity conflicts, spillover conflicts, and sporadic law enforcement operations by third parties', (2009) 91(873) IRRC 127, at 137.
6. Additional Protocol I 1977 to the Geneva Conventions 1949, art. 51; International Committee of the Red Cross (ICRC), 'Rule 1. The Principle of Distinction between Civilians and Combatants'.
7. Additional Protocol I, art. 58(c); ICRC, 'Rule 22. Principle of Precautions against the Effects of Attacks'.
8. Additional Protocol I, art. 50(1).
9. ICRC, 'Rule 3. Definition of Combatants'.
10. CRC, 'Interpretive Guidance on the Notion of Direct Participation in Hostilities under International Humanitarian Law', 2009, at 33.
11. ICRC, 'Rule 6. Civilians' Loss of Protection from Attack'.
12. Interpretive Guidance, at 46.
13. ICRC, 'Rule 14. Proportionality in Attack'.
14. "The Civilian Impact of Drones: Unexamined Costs, Unanswered Questions," Center for Civilians in Conflict and Human Rights Clinic at Columbia Law School (2012), at 8-9.
15. Brian Glyn Williams, "Inside the Murky World of 'Signature Strikes' and the Killing of Americans With Drones", *Huffington Post*, May 31, 2013, accessed May 24, 2016, http://www.huffingtonpost.com/brian-glyn-williams/nside-the-murky-world-of-_b_3367780.html
16. Jo Becker and Scott Shane, "Secret 'Kill List' Proves a Test of Obama's Principles and Will", *The New York Times*, May 29, 2012, accessed May 24, 2016, http://www.nytimes.com/2012/05/29/world/obamas-leadership-in-war-on-al-qaeda.html?_r=0
17. Reaching Critical Will, *'Fully Autonomous Weapons'*.
18. R. Arkin, 'Ethical Robots in Warfare', *Georgia Institute of Technology* (2009).
19. ICCPR, art. 1; ECHR, art. 1.
20. Human Rights Committee, 'General Comment 31', UN Doc. CCPR/C/21/Rev.1/Add.13 (2004).
21. B. van Schaack, "The United States' Position on the Extraterritorial Application of Human Rights Obligations: Now is the Time for Change" *International Legal Studies* 20 (2014) 90.
22. Legality of the Threat or Use of Nuclear Weapons, para. 25.
23. European Convention on Human Rights 1950, art. 2; International Covenant on Civil and Political Rights 1966, art. 6.
24. HRC Res. 25/22, 28 March 2014.
25. Responsibility of States for Internationally Wrongful Acts 2001, art. 16.
26. Rome Statute 1998.

UNMANNED   ARCHITECTURE AND SECURITY SERIES

Twenty-First Century Birdwatching
Ruben Pater

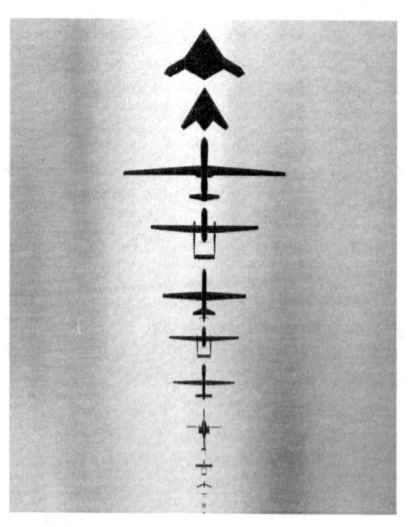

'A Study into 21st Century Drone Acoustics,' an auditive investigation by composer Gonçalo F. Cardoso and designer Ruben Pater

Our first ancestors could tell a lot from looking at the sky. Spotting and recognizing birds provided crucial information about the weather, where to find food, and what predators were near. In the urban landscape of the twenty-first century, our knowledge of the natural environment has been replaced by knowledge of technology. Most of us can't tell the difference between the call of an osprey or a hawk, but everyone can tell the difference between a Nokia ringtone and an iPhone one. We have grown so accustomed to technology that we perceive it as our natural habitat. Drones are quickly becoming a new species in this environment. The American Federal Aviation Administration predicted that by 2030, thirty thousand commercial and government drones could be flying over the U.S. skies. The military seems to anticipate this changing relation with nature and technology in naming its drones: Global Hawk, Heron, Killer Bee, Mantis, Predator, Reaper, Raven, Sentinel, Scan Eagle, and so on. Electronic birds hovering in the air, circling over warzones, until they spot a prey and attack.

Loss of Link

It is important we learn to identify drones by sight and by ear and adapt to this changing environment. But we also have to learn about drone behavior. When a pilot is in control, the drone behaves like any other aircraft. When control is lost, a drone can behave erratically or unethically, and become a danger to friend or foe. For example, when an Irish peacekeeping drone flying over Chad lost its link with the pilot in 2008, it automatically set course for Ireland. Since it had not been reprogrammed to return to its base in Africa, it crashed somewhere in the Sahara after running out of fuel, without ever making it home. A more serious case of a "drone gone rogue" story happened in 2009, when a fully armed drone was flying westbound over Afghanistan and lost the link with the pilot. The U.S. Air Force was forced to shoot it down, in order to prevent the drone from flying into Iranian airspace and unknowingly unleashing a war. The satellite link from the drone to the pilot is its lifeline, the only part that is still human. This prevents drones from being able to fly over the North or South Pole, something that piloted aircraft can do. Since data links rely on communication satellites over the equator, these remote areas are simply out of reach. The detachment of body and soul means a crashed drone is just a wreck. Piloted aircraft that crash are mourned and its pilots remembered as heroes. When a drone crashes the pilot can fluently switch to another drone, a new body.

UNMANNED ARCHITECTURE AND SECURITY SERIES

Crashed MQ1 Predator drone.
Photo: Courtesy of U.S. Air Force

Smile detection. Photo: Nikon, courtesy Ruben Pater

Surveillance in Full-HD

"They don't get hungry. They are not afraid. They don't forget their orders. They don't care if the guy next to them has been shot. Will they do a better job than humans? Yes," explains a Pentagon official in *Wired for War*. It's true; drones can fly up to thirty-three-hour missions, while pilots cannot fly longer than ten hours. A new crew simply takes over, and the drone can stay in flight. Future drones running on solar energy are even designed to be in a permanent state of flight. Their endurance, alongside their sensor technology, makes them the perfect surveillance weapon. They carry high-definition digital cameras, infrared cameras, and they can be fitted with a Gorgon Stare sensor. Named after the Greek myth of three sisters whose gaze could turn to stone, the Gorgon Stare gives us a peek into the future of surveillance. Its 1.8 billion-pixel camera can cover an area of sixteen square kilometres, allowing to identify individuals within the area of a small city. Its cameras can follow twelve different targets at the same time. A surveillance team's wet dream, but an analyst's nightmare: the Pentagon has stated drones recorded so much video footage in 2009 alone it would take someone twenty-four years to watch it all. How can you analyze this amount of video? The answer is, again, technology. The U.S. military's research institute, the Defense Advanced Research Projects Agency, is currently working on intelligent visual software that can analyze video footage, and identify suspect behavior, or identify suspects using face recognition. From hours of video, this software is designed to pick out the terrorist, the car thief, and the protester among innocent bystanders. But can software tell the difference between a kid building a sandcastle and a terrorist burrowing a homemade explosive? When drones are increasingly used domestically, we may find ourselves in a state of permanent surveillance where algorithms end up deciding who is a target and who is not.

Mirror Image

How do you resist such invasive technology? In a 2011 BBC report, a U.S. military soldier explained how a particular group of Taliban fighters couldn't be seen at night because they used space blankets. As drones and helicopters use infrared cameras at night, the Taliban found space blankets an effective way to hide body heat, rendering them invisible to these cameras. Developed by the U.S. space agency NASA in 1964, space blankets are thin sheets of Mylar with a metallic reflective agent. Originally designed to insulate satellites, space blankets turned out to be a great way to keep body heat, or to hide it from prying eyes. The use of cheap materials to counter expensive military sensors is exemplary of the tactics used in asymmetric warfare. In this case, both technologies were developed by the same space and defense industry. The mirrored material of the space blanket reminds us that all kinds of surveillance, no matter how advanced, boil down to people watching other people; and no matter how expensive and advanced technologies may be, they do not win wars alone. We find the tactic of the mirror as a weapon again in the Greek myth of the Gorgon sisters, which gave its name to the U.S. Air Force sensor. Like the Taliban, the Greek hero Perseus could only defeat the deadly stare of the Gorgon sisters by using a mirror to deflect their gaze.

Space blanket, courtesy of Ruben Pater

Permanent State of Conflict

Despite their faults, drones have proved very successful for the U.S. military. The ability to wage war with very little casualties, at least on the American side, has dramatically expanded the U.S. drone program. On the African continent alone, the U.S. flies drones from nine known bases. Given the radius of a Reaper drone, the U.S. can effectively reach all corners of the continent, except its ally South Africa. With the ability to fly almost everywhere as long as the host country grants permission, U.S. drones are adopting the role of a global police patrol, able to strike anywhere, anytime. This is shifting the notion of war from a binary state to a fluid state. U.S. drones have attacked locations in Yemen, Libya, Somalia and Mali, all without declaring war. The question is not just how this real-time, ubiquitous robot surveillance will influence our people's behavior: sooner or later, other countries will want the same ability to take out unwanted targets anywhere in the world. Today, more than eighty-seven nations own drones, twenty-six of which boast larger ones, equivalent to the MQ-1-Predator. For instance, Russia has been very

Friedrich der Große als Perseus, Christian Bernhard Rode, 1789, courtesy of Ruben Pater

UNMANNED   ARCHITECTURE AND SECURITY SERIES

Using the *Drone Survival Guide*, 2014.
Photo courtesy of Ruben Pater

critical of U.S. drone policy, but is simultaneously developing its own eight-billion-dollar drone program. With Western countries supporting or condoning the U.S. drone program to take out targets anywhere it sees fit, we are creating a precedent for other military powers. This is much like saying that sovereignty and the laws of war do not necessarily apply anymore when we label the enemy as terrorists.

Drone Survival Guide

In 2012 I created the *Drone Survival Guide*, a document that shows the silhouettes of the twenty-seven best-known military drones, all to scale, and lists the countries that use them. It also lists a series of countermeasures on how to avoid detection and disrupt the drones' sensors. The guide can be folded and carried with you at all times; printed on metallic coated paper, the front side of the document can be used to reflect sunlight and blind the drones' camera—one of the listed countermeasures. The guide can be downloaded, printed and distributed freely by anyone. Originally published in English and Pashto, people are invited to contribute new translations of the countermeasures, which are currently posted online in thirty-two languages. The *Drone*

TWENTY-FIRST CENTURY BIRDWATCHING

Survival Guide is not useful for survival, anti-drone warfare, nor is it an act of anti-American propaganda. It is made with the sole purpose of sharing information about a phenomenon that is quickly changing warfare, and which many do not yet fully understand. The *Drone Survival Guide* is a civilian initiative, self-funded and made with public information, to balance the information provided by actors with a political or commercial agenda.

dronesurvivalguide.org

UNMANNED ARCHITECTURE AND SECURITY SERIES

Decolonized Skies: Art, the View from Above and the Formation of New Civil Knowledge
Yael Messer, Gilad Reich

In 2013, movie star George Clooney announced that he would devote all of his Nespresso campaign earnings to fund the Satellite Sentinel Project, which uses a civilian satellite to document war crimes committed during the Sudanese civil war. Clooney's announcement gave rise to some justified concerns about the delicate dynamics between good intentions, big money and civilian use in military technologies. Who decides where and how these satellite images will be circulated? What about the privacy of the Sudanese people, who might not wish to be subjected to constant surveillance? And what is the legal, moral, and ethical status of such images, whose production is based on strategies identified with the history of colonial oppression and control? In a step that helped alleviate these concerns, Clooney partnered with the human rights organization Enough Project; although this gave the project moral validity, it did not solve all of its inherent contradictions.

The case of Satellite Sentinel Project stands out because it involves a celebrity who can communicate a human rights struggle to large audiences across the world. However, its underlying conception—the use of technological innovation to demilitarize the aerial perspective and use it as a means of producing and circulating civilian knowledge—has been gaining momentum in recent years. Just as Clooney joined forces with a human rights organization, artists, scientists, scholars, designers, journalists,

DECOLONIZED SKIES

architects, and activists also collaborate and form transdisciplinary research and action groups. These groups extract aerial space from the control of the state—and the authoritarian perspective that comes along with it—, offering alternative ways of producing, analyzing, and circulating aerial imagery. The images presented in this text provide a glimpse into the modus operandi and practices of these groups and individuals, and point at the historical origins of civilian aerial image.

The presented projects are to a large degree a reaction to the appropriation of the sky and aerial perspective by European colonial powers from late nineteenth century onwards: the view from above allowed these powers to catalog and organize geographic territories while ignoring the culture and needs of local population. The remote perspective of the view from above, which for the most part removes humans from the photo—or at the very least minimizes their presence—, has been conducive to military control on the ground. As photography and film scholar, Paula Amad, notes in a 2012 essay for *History of Photography*,[1] the institutional use of aerial photographs has transformed the view from above into a signifier of control, surveillance, and violence. However, the vast interest generated in recent years in the demilitarization of the view from above also stems from two relatively new and concurrent processes. The first is the growing use of digital navigation and orientation systems such as Global Positioning System (GPS) and Google Earth. These orientation technologies, which were developed in the military sphere and are subjected to governmental monitoring, have become

Satellite Sentinel Project, screen capture

UNMANNED   ARCHITECTURE AND SECURITY SERIES

Antonov An-26 over Tira Mande village, South Kordofan. A satellite image, highlighting a Sudanese bomber, that Clooney used in his March 15 testimony before a Senate committee. Source: DigitalGlobe.
https://www.flickr.com/photos/enoughproject/

inseparable from our everyday lives, considerably changing our relation to maps and the reality they strive to portray. The second process is the dramatic rise in the use of drones for monitoring, surveillance, and combat since 9/11. In fact, most airstrikes in areas of conflict such as Afghanistan, Yemen and Gaza, are performed by drones. In Pakistan, for instance, over two thousand and four hundred people have been killed by drones in the last five years—Obama's years in office—according to a report by journalist Jack Serle.[2] These two trends are not mutually exclusive; on the contrary, they are intertwined, as part of a comprehensive process in which the lines between the military and the civilian, the local and the global, become progressively blurred.

On the whole, Clooney's project is centralized and conservative, in the mode of image production—satellite image—, analysis—by a group of experts—, and circulation—the image analysis is distributed to mainstream media outlets and international law organizations. At the other end of the spectrum, we find the Grassroots Mapping project of the organization PublicLab—an online community of artists, scholars, activists, and technology practitioners. Established in 2010, the project is entirely collaborative: local groups are invited to work together on an issue that directly concerns their surroundings, building DIY aerial cameras out of everyday materials such as kites, balloons, rubber bands or plastic bottles, and taking multiple aerial photographs. Open source software developed by the organization allows these amateur photographers to "knit" the images into a map and mark it in a way that is best suited to their needs. This practice facilitates the production of autonomous, local geographic knowledge and helps uncover the spatial power relations that shape the lives of the people taking these photographs. At the same time, it also reintroduces people to aerial photography by giving them control over the manufacturing of the image, its interpretation and usage. Thus, for example, in a project led by the scholar and activist Hagit Keysar and the artist Zemer Sat, children in East Jerusalem's Silwan neighborhood learned to create independent aerial photographs that express their point of view on their surroundings, while simultaneously circumventing the ban on collecting data where freedom of movement and access to information are hindered.[3]

Most of the projects that engage with the demilitarization of the view from above exist somewhere in this range—between Sudan and Silwan, the satellite and the kite, centralization and collaboration, specialists and residents, and between one point of view aimed "there" and myriad dispersed perspectives that look towards "here." While some of the projects are on the activist side of the spectrum, focusing on action rather than representation, other projects stress the potential for a new visual language, extricating aerial photography from of its associations with the notions of control and monitoring.

Aerial photography has grappled with issues of citizenship, obedience, and empowerment from its inception. The French photographer and caricaturist Nadar, who was the first to take aerial photographs from a hot air balloon in 1858, declined the French armed forces' offer to conduct reconnaissance photos behind enemy lines. The American camera inventor and aviation expert George R. Lawrence, who worked several decades later, did collaborate occasionally with the United States military. However, he is famous mostly for his independent series of photographs documenting San Francisco after the 1906 earthquake that left the city in ruins. This series of photographs is one of the first examples of the power of aerial photography to provide real-time documentation on a specific event, serving as the main tool for knowledge production and analysis from a civilian perspective.

The Golden Age of "pre-modern civilian photography," as author Paula Amad has dubbed it, only lasted three more years, ending in 1909, when the French air force started taking aerial photographs on a regular basis, building on the knowledge accumulated by pioneers of photography such as Nadar and Lawrence. Soon the aerial perspective became a "state-controlled space," synonymous with monitoring and regulation. Even in the years following the Second World War, when aerial perspective was harnessed towards the organization of the urban space, the state did not return aerial photography to the control of those who were being photographed. Urban planning, like the colonial gaze before it, has engaged in the division and organization of space in a way that serves those who look at it from above, mostly not allowing the representation of the complex social relations that exist in any inhabited area. Only in the early 1980s, with the rise of satellite technology, artists and activists once again tried to reclaim the view from above—this time as civilians, collaborating with other civilians towards civilian goals.

The pioneers of this shift were without a doubt Ocean Earth, led by the artist Peter Fend. In the early 1980s, Fend partnered with a series of scientists specializing in satellite data analysis and activists who monitored geo-political disaster areas around the globe in order to purchase satellite imagery. They bought images from the Earth Resources Observation and Science (EROS) satellite, a governmental entity that also provides commercial services. Ocean Earth's declared aim was to conduct an independent analysis of disaster areas and sell their findings

DECOLONIZED SKIES

Disaster of the balloon "Le Géant" at "Nieubourg" near Hanover in 1863, by Henry de Montaut. Source: Wikimedia Commons

to leading media outlets in the U.S. This was Fend's way of fighting mainstream media from the inside: he wanted to sell the stories that the military and the government were covering, and leave them no other choice than to publish information that had a substantial journalistic value. Fend and his team exposed, *inter alia*, the British armed forces deployment around the Falkland Islands in 1982—which Britain had tried to keep secret from its citizens—, and were the first to point at the continuing leak of radioactive materials from the Chernobyl nuclear reactor in 1986—information that the Soviets wished to hide from the world. As an artist, Fend emphasized color analysis and the ability to read abstract imagery as essential tools in deciphering aerial images.

In the last couple of years, Ocean Earth's preoccupation with abstract concerns and questions of visibility in the context of aerial perspective analysis has become more prominent, mostly due to the growing use of drones by artists. As artists like Trevor Paglen and Thomas van Houtryve stress in their works, the view from above is a deceptive view, since it gives the illusion of objectivity whereas the process of deciphering the blurry image is based on preexisting knowledge and assumptions. In military satellite images, for instance, each photograph is accompanied by a document detailing the spatial context of the photograph and what is seen in it. In the 2007-2011 series of photographs *The Other Night Sky*,[4] Paglen photographed reconnaissance satellites and space debris floating above the Earth. The information about the satellites was gathered by a global network of amateur "satellite watchers", who tracked the orbit of each satellite. Paglen used state-of-the-art photography equipment to capture the satellites in their orbit, and yet, the photographs he produced are to a large degree abstract. With that, Paglen confronts the viewer with one of the distinguishing properties of aerial photography, described by author Laura Kurgan as "measurable and digital, uncentered and ambiguous, yet comprehensive and authoritative." Van Houtryve also engages with the discrepancy between what we see and what we think we see, using a thoroughly different artistic strategy: in the 2013 photographic series *Blue Sky Days*,[5] he wandered across the United States with a drone, photographing social events similar to those during which U.S. forces attacked civilians in Pakistan: weddings, funerals, and social gatherings. A military report that describes a strike on civilians during a prayer in a mosque's yard, for instance, was translated in the American context to an aerial photograph of people practicing yoga in a park. The similarities between the subjects' body language as it appears in the report and the body language of the people in the yoga class engenders confusion, reminding us the dangerous and manipulative potential embodied in aerial photographs, and the degree to which they require ideological and cultural interpretation that will imbue them with meaning.

Questions of proximity, perception and visibility also emerge from works that employ global locating and mapping systems. One example is the 2011 project *Elements of Composition*[6] by the Dutch artist duo, Bik van der Pol, which engages with the urban development of southeast Manhattan in New York. In a parking lot located in the heart of the neighborhood, one of the last spaces in the area that is not covered by high-rise buildings, the artists created a text piece in massive dimensions, which could only be read from the air. In collaboration with Google Earth, they photographed the parking lot with the aim of incorporating the documentation in the company's digital archive. At the same time, they also arranged guided tours in which residents and urban planning experts discussed the future of the neighborhood in general and the rights to vertical development in particular. In this series of works, both from the air and at street level, the artists underscore the dialectic aspect of the view from above, which comes into being only through its interplay with the human point of view from the ground, and attempt to counter the act of erasing people from the photograph.[7]

In a later stage of the same project, Bik van der Pol presented another satellite image of the same site, which they bought from a private company. The juxtaposition of the two images reveals how the artists manipulated the previous Google image, and merely re-wrote the text piece using Photoshop. However, these manipulations remain unbeknownst to the viewer. Only through a comparison between the two images can we understand the problematic status of the aerial image when it is produced by a commercial corporation that aims to meet both aesthetic and market conventions.

Ocean Earth made another significant contribution to the demilitarization of the view from above, which concerns the manner in which the image is created and analyzed. As mentioned above, Peter Fend did not work alone. The breakthroughs achieved by the group's analysis of ecological and political disasters were made possible thanks to the collaboration between artists, activists, scientists, and designers. Over the years, this multidisciplinary model of sharing became the model preferred by activists who engage in the formation of civilian knowledge. The Bureau for Inverse Technology, led by Australian engineer and scientist Natalie Jeremijenko, started engaging with the subversive potential of the use of drones as early as 1997. The Bureau flew a radio-controlled model aircraft, equipped with a micro-video

'Suspect behaviour,' from the series Blue Sky Days,
Tomas van Houtryve

Elements of composition [As above, so below],
Bik van der Pol, 2011

camera and transmitter, over campuses of Silicon Valley companies that develop aerial control technologies. The common denominator of all these campuses was their status as a no-camera zone—a precaution against information leakage. The act of photographing them from the air brought to the fore the close link between visibility, knowledge, and the aerial perspective.

Similarly, a highly relevant contemporary example is the *Drone Strikes* project lead by the group Forensic Architecture, which has been working since 2011 under the guidance of researcher and architect Eyal Weizman at the Goldsmiths, University of London. This research group comprises "spatial activists"—architects, computer scientists, fieldworkers and activists—who reconstruct deadly drone strikes in conflict areas, in order to identify patterns linking a specific architectural space to a particular kind of aerial military attacks, and uncover what satellite imagery does not reveal. Here too, people return to aerial photography by collecting testimonies of survivors: these testimonies are translated by Forensic Architecture into three-dimensional simulation videos, that can serve as evidence in courts and can be used by international human rights organizations.

A portion of Forensic Architecture's activity is devoted to incidents in Israel and Palestine, an activity that we see as holding particular importance for several reasons. Throughout the twentieth century, Palestine and Israel were photographed extensively from the air; author Norma Musih recounts how this effort was first conducted during the First World War by the British Royal Flying Corps and the Bavarian unit of the German Luftstreitkräfte; the years that followed saw this kind of documentation performed by the State of Israel. The non-military knowledge stored in these photographs only recently started attracting scholarly attention, and Forensic Architecture's future projects may shed additional light on the civilian uses that can be derived from the history of aerial photography in Israel and Palestine. Furthermore, in recent years Israel has become one of the world's largest drone manufacturers: according to various sources, in 2013 Israel defense industries sold more drones than the United States. One of the reasons for the tremendous success of Israeli technology is the fact that its drones are considered "combat-proven": as reported by author Markus Becker,[8] Israel uses Gaza and other places in the Middle East as a testing ground for new aerial attack technologies, and then maximizes the profits from their sale.

A commercial air show targeting the international market, scheduled to open in Israel several months after *Operation Protective Edge* and the writing of this essay in 2014, will be devoted to the central role that unmanned technologies served in the Operation, particularly to the central part of combat drones made in Israel. The air show's website as well as several reports indicate that the event's program includes the screening of videos documenting aerial strikes conducted during the Operation, offering live demonstrations of new technologies implemented in it, and launching a new model of the Hermes drone, the "star" of Israel defense industries and one of the most resilient working assault aerial vehicles in the world.[9]

In light of these developments, as well as the total media blackout imposed by the Israeli government on any information that concerns the use of drones in combat and killing, a critical examination of the subject gains added urgency. As the images presented here demonstrate, the collaboration between artists, human rights activists, scientists and scholars from different disciplines can offer an outlook that exposes the violent mechanisms with which the state appropriates the view from above, and simultaneously time proposes civilian alternatives for its demilitarization.

1. Paula Amad. "From God's-eye to Camera-eye: Aerial Photography's Post-humanist and Neo-humanist Visions of the World," *History of Photography* 36(1) (2012), 66—86.
2. Jack Serle. "Drone Warfare," The Bureau of Investigative Journalism, January 23, 2014, accessed May 25, 2016, http://tinyurl.com/mr3wgpf
3. See: Hagit Keysar, "Aerial Photography: Community" *Maftehakh, Lexical Review of Political Thought 7* (2014), 205-232. In Hebrew.
4. See http://www.paglen.com
5. See: tomasvh.com
6. See: http://www.bikvanderpol.net
7. See Jason Farman. "Mapping the Digital Empire: Google Earth and the Process of Postmodern Cartography," *New Media Society 12* (2010), 872.
8. Markus Becker. "Factory and Lab: Israel's War Business," Spiegel Online International, August 27, 2014, accessed May 24, 2016, http://www.spiegel.de/international/world/defense-industry-the-business-of-war-in-israel-a-988245.html
9. See the air show's website: ausr.i-hls.com

UNMANNED ARCHITECTURE AND SECURITY SERIES

Life of a Drone Pilot
Francesca Recchia

Cyber warfare, particularly drone warfare, is the object of ongoing heated debate. Critics point to its heavy human and financial costs. For supporters, however, drones are an accurate and cost-effective means of conducting war.

Sarah Holewinski, executive director of the NGO, Center for Civilians in Conflict, and Larry Lewis, an adviser to the U.S. Joint Chiefs of Staff, recently conducted a study based on classified material, which reveals that contrary to U.S. President Barack Obama's claims, drones kill ten times more civilians than manned jet fighters.

Among the causes highlighted by the study is the insufficient training provided to pilots. This is driven, in part, by the lengthy time required to fully prepare aviators and the urgency with which they are needed.

Discussions around cyber warfare and the dehumanization of war seem, however, to forget the existence of these pilots, who make choices, take decisions, and are accountable for their actions.

Cyberwar has drastically changed the nature of such accountability and the actual role that soldiers' bodies and physical strength play in war.

Albert Hibpshman is a United States Air Force (USAF) pilot of manned and unmanned aircrafts. During his recent deployment to Afghanistan, Hibpshman was a Mission Commander flying MC-12ws—intelligence, surveillance and reconnaissance aircrafts

LIFE OF A DRONE PILOT

—as well as a Group Liaison Officer, responsible for the coordination between five flying squadrons and Army, Marine and special forces units at bases spread throughout southern Afghanistan.

In this interview, Hibpshman gives his personal take and experience with contemporary drone warfare, and the human component of cyber warfare.

> **Francesca Recchia (FR)** How did you become a drone pilot? What brings a pilot to leave behind planes and helicopters and start flying Unmanned Aerial Vehicles (UAVs)?

Albert Hibpshman (AH) My USAF career began in pilot training, flying trainer aircraft with my instructors. After a year of training I went off to learn how to fly the KC-135 tanker aircraft [an aerial refueling military plane]. I spent three years flying over Iraq and Afghanistan, supporting Aeromedical Evacuations and test programs. Being gone three-quarters of the time with a new wife and then a baby at home was hard on me. I volunteered to fly unmanned aircraft and since there were few pilots interested in UAVs at the time, I was moved shortly thereafter to one of the new squadrons to start training. My regular time at home, even after long days, gave me an opportunity to spend more time with my wife and be a part of my child's life. At the same time, I was able to progress through the ranks, become a flight commander, instructor and volunteer as is expected from all good USAF officers.

> **FR** Drones represent a radical shift in the modes of warfare. What kind of training did you undergo to become a drone pilot?

AH Training to learn the aircraft systems, sensors and communication systems is critical to understanding how to employ an unmanned aircraft on a military mission. We are trained in each of those areas, capitalizing on previous experience in manned aircraft. Training that includes being aware of aircraft programmed "communications out" flight paths and altitude, as well as regularly updating those programs, are new habits that must become second nature.

    FR Which habits and notions did you carry with you from your previous, "traditional" military experience?

AH An aggressive cross check and skepticism are healthy habits that I've brought from previous manned aircraft flying. Respect for the aircraft and performance limitations as well as an understanding of the weather and how to work around it are essential to accomplish the mission under demanding circumstances.

    FR What would you say are the main skills required to be a good drone pilot?

AH Drone pilots need to be good at multi-tasking, have a good understanding of what the aircraft should be doing and able to perform a quick cross check to see if it is in fact at the right place, going the right direction, at the correct altitude since there are no "seat of the pants" cues to alert pilots of a change. We need to work with our sensor operators to ensure the mission is being accomplished, while troubleshooting communications issues and working with the distributed ground crew for processing, exploitation and distribution of mission products. As a mission commander, I make every effort to allow my crew to excel and only interrupt them if something isn't going according to plan, or if the plan changes.

    FR There has recently been an acknowledgment by the Armed Forces Health Surveillance Center that a very high percentage of drone pilots are victims of post-traumatic stress disorders. Is there any kind of psychological training that you receive? Do you have dedicated and specialized professional support and counseling while you are deployed?

LIFE OF A DRONE PILOT

AH Our counseling is mostly self-initiated. There are counselors available to us, even while deployed, but we have to seek them out when we need help, want to talk or are unsure how to handle our reactions to a situation.

> **FR** I am quite fascinated by the particular understanding of distance and proximity that drone pilots experience. You may be thousands of miles apart from your target and yet incredibly close to it. You may be observing your target for days and weeks, learn about his habits and daily routines and yet be on a different continent altogether. How do you manage this?

AH I have to remember that I am a military officer, called on to execute a mission. Intel briefs us on the specifics of why an individual needs to be killed or captured, so we know why the mission is being carried out. I suppose we get used to working with the Army to carry out their objectives without getting emotionally involved.

> **FR** On a similar note, when you follow a target for a very long time and develop an almost intimate knowledge of his life, how is to execute your orders and press the trigger? Does this physical distance but visual proximity make it any harder?

AH I personally have never been asked to fire munitions, though the folks I've talked to who have say they know the objective and reason why they must be neutralized, making it easier to "pull the trigger."

> **FR** How do you deal with the physical distance from your target? Does war feel different from behind a computer screen?

AH Physical distance can make it difficult to work in real time with troops on the ground, especially if communications are not clear or readily available. Computer screens, whether in the aircraft orbiting overhead or in a Ground Control Station, are equally real.

> **FR** Combat planes or helicopters often have architectural objects or locales as targets, whereas drones–because of their precision–may have a specific person as a target. How do you deal with the risk of collateral damage and with the potential margins of mistake?

AH The local Ground Force Commander assesses the risk associated with target and the aircraft commander only strikes when given the order.

> **FR** War stinks. What does flying a drone smell like?

AH Deployments for USAF pilots can be challenging and often involve spending as much time away as we are at home. For the "drone pilot", we work twelve-hour shifts, often during the night, on many weekends and holidays. A new challenge I face is that I'm vulnerable to be on the schedule every holiday or on wing safety down days [days of no flying where the entire base reviews flight safety, maintenance and other safety procedures]. Rest must be carefully planned or it is hard to get.

> **FR** Do you miss seeing the clouds from above?

AH Yes. Like many unmanned aircraft pilots I spend time flying for fun by renting an airplane and going up with family or friends.

First published on Muftah on July 12, 2013

Discussion

Landscapes of Secrecy: Data and Reporting in the Drone Debate

PANEL
LANDSCAPES OF SECRECY:
Data and Reporting in the Drone Debate

180 VARICK ST., SUITE 1610,
NEW YORK, NY 10014
STUDIOXNYC.COM
@STUDIOXNYC

In collaboration with Bard's Center for the Study of the Drone, this event will look to open a discussion on the gathering/reconstructing of data regarding US Drone strikes, placing in conversation three researchers from diverse disciplinary backgrounds to talk about their attempts to understand and represent the nature and extent of U.S. targeted killing operations, the relationship between secrecy and forms of surveillance and violence, and the production of "evidence" at the intersections of legal and physical environments. Moderated by Arthur Holland Michel (Bard) with Bradley Samuels (SITU Studio, Naureen Shah (Amnesty International), and Josh Begley (Metadata+). This will be the second in a Studio-X Global series on *Security Regimes*.

THURSDAY, APRIL 10, 2014
7:00–8:30 PM

FREE AND OPEN TO THE PUBLIC, NO RSVP REQUIRED

UNMANNED   ARCHITECTURE AND SECURITY SERIES

Landscape of Secrecy: Data and Reporting in the Drone Debate was a collaboration between GSAPP's Studio-X and Bard College's Center for the Study of the Drone (CSD), which aimed to open a discussion on the gathering and reconstructing of data regarding U.S. drone strikes. Researchers from diverse disciplinary backgrounds discussed the strategies to understand and represent the nature and extent of U.S. targeted killing operations and the relationship between secrecy and forms of surveillance and violence.

The discussion was convened and introduced by Carlos-Solis-Keyser, Program Coordinator, Studio-X NYC, and Marina Otero Verzier, Director of Global Network Programming at Studio-X/ GSAPP. Dan Gettinger and Arthur Holland Mitchel, co-organizers of this program and founders and co-editors of the CSD, acted as moderators of the panel. The Center is a site of reference for the interdisciplinary study of drones and seeks to contribute to the development of sensible policies to govern drones use.

Bradley Samuels, of SITU Research, interrogated how architects could take part in the done debate as spatial consultants at the intersections of legal and physical environments, and how, together with other practitioners, they could contribute to the production of "evidence" and high resolution data on the strikes.

Naureen Shah, Legislative Counsel at the American Civil Liberties Union, unpacked the complex territory of the drone program and its articulation with international law, human rights and technology. She examined the dangers of abstraction and fetishization of quantitative information in the representation of the drone strikes, and pointed out how witness testimony reminds us that when we when we talk about data, we are really talking about civilian casualties.

Data artist Josh Begley discussed the ambiguity of technology in its relationship with knowledge and power. He shared his experience in developing the application Metadata+, which has transformed any iPhone in a device for tracking every reported United States drone strike.

Infrastructures of Secrecy and Public Knowledge
Dan Gettinger, Arthur Holland Mitchel

In this panel, we set out to examine the place where the infrastructures of secrecy that have been built around the CIA's targeted killing campaign meets public knowledge of, and interest in the issue. Despite over a decade of drone strikes, the Obama Administration only recently admitted that it does indeed occasionally—and, at times, not so occasionally—kill suspected enemies of the U.S. with drones outside of declared war zones.

Though the administration refuses to release any details about the four-hundred-plus deadly missions that it has carried out with drones outside of declared war zones, our knowledge of the extent and scope of the program is not solely speculative. In fact, the public does have a great deal of information about how many strikes have occurred, where they have occurred, and whom they have killed. We have three organizations in particular to thank for this: The Bureau of Investigative Journalism, the New America Foundation and the Long War Journal. Much of this information has been collected by the three main wire services, AP, AFP and Reuters, as well as a few regional media outlets.

That being said, the information that we do have is by no means perfect. In fact, it is deeply flawed, at times to the point of being useless. While the information that we have about drone strikes is comprehensive, it is divergent and, at time, contradictory.

Estimates of the number of civilians killed in drone strikes, for example, vary wildly depending on the methodology and sources one uses to count.

The imperfect nature of the data set, coupled with the administration's narrative that these operations are secret because it is in the interest of our security to keep them secret, has greatly hindered our ability to develop a robust popular dialogue around the issue. While drones have indeed captured a great deal of media attention, the policy discussion—the nitty-gritty, so to speak—remains woefully lacking. It is difficult to engage in a policy debate when the public's knowledge of the details of that policy is speculative. At the Center, we believe that good public information is prerequisite to a coherent public policy debate. We do not, as an institution, take a stand for or against any particular policy in terms of the use of drones, but we do believe that the more information we have about these uses, the better equipped we will be to decide whether or not we want them.

But until we do see more information, we need to make the information that we do have as meaningful as possible. The challenge is not just how to effectively collect and organize imperfect information; it's also how to present that information in such a way that will make people care. These two tasks are intimately connected, and striking a balance between the two can be extremely difficult—simplify the analysis too much, and it becomes meaningless; add too much complexity and the public will lose interest. Navigating this landscape of secrecy is central to advancing the public discussion about the use of lethal drones.

Landscapes of Secrecy: Discussion

April 10, 2014
Studio-X, New York City

Arthur Holland Michel (AHM) We're here to talk about how to deal with a deeply imperfect data set. We have a targeted killing regime that has been going on for over a decade now, but we don't have reliable data because the U.S. government chooses not to release statistics on its CIA drone operations. There are three organizations that really look at the statistics of drones strikes. The Bureau of Investigative Journalism, the New America Foundation and the Long War Journal. They count civilian and combatant casualties. The count civilian casualties as a proportion of the total casualties caused by drone strikes. The Bureau has calculated that the proportion is between twelve percent and thirt-five percent civilian casualties. The New America Foundation numbers put the proportion at between eight and fifteen percent. The Long War Journal puts it at six percent. That gives you a sense of how imperfect the data is. Those ranges are so large so as to make the data almost abstract, in a sense.

We're here to look at how we can deal with that, how to represent that data and how to have a substantive conversation given these limitations. We have three people here who have very different methodologies for how to approach the issue. Naureen Shah is the legislative council at the ACLU. She has been involved in several very influential reports on drone warfare, both with Amnesty International and the Human Rights Clinic at Columbia University. Bradley Samuels is a partner at SITU Research, which has developed an online platform to present UN special rapporteur Ben Emmerson's recent report on drone strikes. Josh Begley is a data artist and is responsible for Dronestream, which you may have heard of; in 2012 Josh decided to tweet every single drone strike that had ever happened. It took him a lot longer than he thought it was going to take, but it drew a lot of attention to the issue. He is also the creator of Metadata+, which is a phone app for tracking drone strikes.

Naureen Shah (NS) Why are we so obsessed about visualizing and collecting data on drone strike killings? What does it really matter to the larger debate on drones? We know that there have been more than four thousand people killed in about four hundred drone strikes, a lot of them occurring since 2008 under the Bush Administration and the Obama Administration. We have these raw numbers. Determining who these people are has been critical to our ability to discuss the strikes, because the larger context is a debate about who is being killed. If you told me four hundred people were disappeared or kidnapped, and that four thousand people had been tortured, I could tell you that was a mass case of human rights violations. But if you tell me that four thousand people have been killed and they've been killed in a part of the world where there is armed conflict, as in Afghanistan where there are armed groups locally operating, it's a more complicated story. It's not just a case of a human rights abuse—it could be case of a justifiable killing. But here's the problem: the Obama Administration, in waging a pretty extensive campaign of air strikes, has tried to maintain secrecy about who's being killed. And instead of explaining who's being killed, in terms of providing the data, they've told a story. And the narrative is essentially that the right people are being killed and everyone else is doing fine, except in a few instances that the administration won't disclose.

As an advocate working on these issues, and as a researcher reporting on drone strike killings, I've witnessed three periods. The first, starting around 2009 or 2010, was a period of initial, scattered reports about drone strikes that were occurring in increasing frequency. These reports alerted a lot of us in the community that something was going on here that wasn't just spillover from the Afghanistan conflict, something different. And during that time all we really had was media reports. These were reports were filed by journalists who were operating in the areas where drone strikes occur, but they weren't necessarily getting access to the "scene of the crimes," if you will. And what we'd have there is maybe three or four reporters working and providing details to a national or international media outlet. Say three of those journalists claim five people killed were all militants, and one of those journalists says that actually many people were killed, and some of them were civilians. The story that you would see reported in the Associated Press and eventually *The New York Times* would be that everyone killed was a militant. Even the term militant itself was not really queried until recently.

The second stage was the development of reporting on who was being killed. The Bureau of Investigative Journalism, the Long War Journal, and the New America Foundation decided to take all of those scattered media reports and put them into a database in order to tell a story about the overall number of people being killed and, who those people were, whether they were civilians or militants. This is when the Obama Administration started to go on an offensive against the very notion that civilians are being killed. Instead of saying a few people have been killed who were civilians, the administration starts saying that zero people have been killed. Instead of the credible reports about civilian deaths leading the administration to acknowledge that civilians have been killed, we see the opposite. We see denial, which is actually not uncommon. When human rights groups confront governments about abuses, they usually either deny that the abuse is happening, or say that the people who have been abused deserved it. In this case, we really see both responses. The U.S. government is not willing to provide the facts, and they say that most of the people who have been killed are senior members of al Qaeda.

The third stage, which has been the last few years, has seen organizations like the Associated Press and particular journalists devote a lot of resources to on-the-ground investigations, providing really strong documentation of particular drone strikes. That's what Amnesty International decided to do for its most recent report. Amnesty reviewed all forty-five strikes that happened in Pakistan between January 2012 and August 2013. And of those forty-five strikes we were able to document nine in depth. And of those nine, four raised serious concerns about violations of the right to life. We were trying to show documentation of particular instances and show those to the government. While the government could continue to say that the numbers that these organizations are basing their assessments on are wrong, it can't summarily dismiss facts that were detailed in the investigations, using satellite imagery, video footage, and with multiple teams having been sent in to interview people.

It was in this way that we investigated the killing of a grandmother named Mamana Bibi. Let me read it to you.

> "Accustomed to seeing drones overhead, Mamana Bibi and her grandchildren continued their daily routine. "The drone planes were flying over our village all day and night, flying in pairs sometimes three together. We had grown used to them flying over our village all the time," Zubair Rehman continued. "I was watering our animals and my brother was harvesting maize crop," said Nabeela.
>
> Then, before her family's eyes, Mamana Bibi was blown into pieces by at least two Hellfire missiles fired concurrently from a U.S. drone aircraft.
>
> There was a very bad smell and the area was full of smoke and dust. I couldn't breathe properly for several

LANDSCAPES OF SECRECY: DISCUSSION

The son and grandchildren of Mamana Bibi, a 68-year-old
Pakistani woman allegedly killed in a U.S. drone strike, display family pictures.
Courtesy Amnesty International

minutes," said Zubair. "The explosion was very close to us. It was very strong, it took me into the air and pushed me onto the ground," added Nabeela. She later ventured to where her grandmother had been picking vegetables earlier in the day. "I saw her shoes. We found her mutilated body a short time afterwards," recalled Nabeela. "It had been thrown quite a long distance away by the blast and it was in pieces. We collected as many different parts from the field and wrapped them in a cloth."

This is a testimonial method of building human rights reports. We try to humanize the people that we're talking about, so we're no longer talking about the categories of "civilian" and "militant," but we're talking about children and a grandmother and really brutal, graphic things like body parts lying on the ground. I'll stop there.

Bradley Samuels (BS) For the past three years we've been working on the Forensic Architecture project, which is being run by Eyal Weizman out of Goldsmiths, University of London. Broadly speaking, the project looks at how data visualization and spatial analysis—tools native to architecture, art and filmmaking—can be leveraged in the service of human rights and international law. It's a very speculative project in that sense, because it seeks to marry fields which otherwise wouldn't be in contact. Each case proceeds as applied research, in the sense that each case we work on is a real case. Each involves a constellation of partners: a human rights organization, legal counsel and ourselves— the architects and artists on the team. The case I'll talk about today is the one specifically focused on drone strikes.

Recently, Ben Emmerson, the UN special *rapporteur* on counterterrorism released his final report on civilian casualties caused by drone strikes. The report sought to identify thirty specific strikes for which there's reason to inquire further into the possibility of civilian deaths. Typically

LANDSCAPES OF SECRECY: DISCUSSION

A/HRC/25/59

Advance Unedited Version

Distr.: General
28 February 2014

Original: English

Human Rights Council
Twenty-fifth session
Agenda item 3
**Promotion and protection of all human rights, civil,
political, economic, social and cultural rights,
including the right to development**

Report of the Special Rapporteur on the promotion and protection of human rights and fundamental freedoms while countering terrorism, Ben Emmerson[*]

Summary

This is the third annual report submitted to the Human Rights Council by the Special Rapporteur on the promotion and protection of human rights and fundamental freedoms while countering terrorism, Ben Emmerson.

In chapter II of the report, the Special Rapporteur lists his key activities undertaken from 10 January to 16 December 2013. In the main report, contained in chapter III, the Special Rapporteur examines the use of remotely piloted aircraft, or drones, in extraterritorial lethal counter-terrorism operations, including in the context of asymmetrical armed conflict, and allegations that the increasing use of remotely piloted aircraft, or drones, has caused disproportionate civilian casualties, and makes recommendations to States. This report constitutes the continuation of the Special Rapporteur's interim report on the use of drones to the General Assembly (A/68/389).

---

[*] Late submission.

GE.14-

Please recycle

UNMANNED   ARCHITECTURE AND SECURITY SERIES

Forensic Architecture. Drone Strikes, Investigating covert operations through spatial media

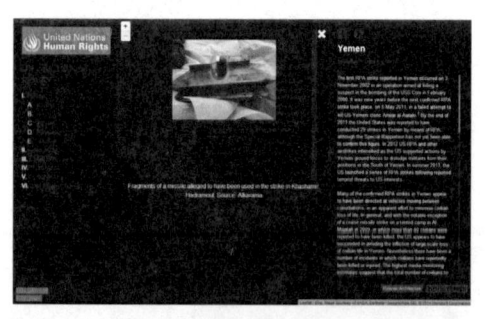

Forensic Architecture. Case study no. 5: Jaar and al Wade'a, Abyan Province, Yemen, 2011

Forensic Architecture. Case study no. 3: Miranshah, North Waziristan, March 30, 2012

82

this is what you get to see from a UN special *rapporteur* at the end of a nine- or twelve-month research period.

It's a PDF, it's usually longform, it's textual and it's read mostly by folks who are very knowledgeable in the subject, such as policy folks and academics. It's not necessarily the most accessible format. What Ben was interested in doing was taking this information and releasing it in two parallel ways. One is the more conventional PDF way and the other is to do it in a multimedia platform, in order to leverage all the different kinds of media that were used in the investigation, which were helpful in understanding the circumstances of each individual strike. In the report he mentions that there's an auxiliary website, our platform. It hosts all the same textual information, along with photographs, spreadsheets, video and testimony. The task was to design a platform that allowed us to synthesize and represent any and all possible types of information.

Because it's so hard to get data on the ground, as Naureen just mentioned, every strike site had different documentation. So you can click on a strike and then you can pull up anything that might be relevant to what happened:

In some cases, it's really just about establishing with

Forensic Architecture. Case study no. 5: Jaar and al Wade'a,
Abyan Province, Yemen, 2011

certainty where the strike occurred. We were in an initial meeting with the Bureau of Investigative Journalism and Reprieve, which is another organization that does really important research on drone strikes, and we said that we had found three different GPS coordinates for a single strike. They were all within six kilometers. If you want to drill in and think about this in as high a resolution as possible, you first have to actually determine the location of the strike with certainty. It prompted our decision to spend four hundred dollars buying satellite imagery and to send someone on the ground to corroborate. In some cases it was actually not possible to determine with certainty where a strike occurred. You can say it's a village of this name, but you can't say exactly where the strike occurred. My point is that that discussion, that debate, that effort is sometimes prompted by the need to examine things in higher resolution.

We found before and after satellite images that actually showed definitively the destroyed buildings.

We looked at network television footage from the ground, looking at street patterns and the size of buildings and trying to look back at satellite imagery and cross reference heights of shadows in order to determine where this occurred.

We used photographs taken on the ground to provide context. Photographs of strike sites themselves. Anything and everything. Pieces of munitions' circuit boards. And Ben was also emphatic that the work should have a human face. Otherwise, the investigation and the representation can quickly become very abstract; we quickly move away from the fact that we're talking about civilian casualties when we talk about data. Witness testimony is always important, not just for details but to give a voice to the victims.

This was the network footage that was used.

A lot of news sources are often referred to in the report. These are a great resource, but an imperfect one. The idea here is to zoom in as much as we can. When I talk about resolutions, it's not just a pixel I'm talking about; it's

LANDSCAPES OF SECRECY: DISCUSSION

Forensic Architecture. Case study no. 5: Jaar and al Wade'a,
Abyan Province, Yemen, 2011

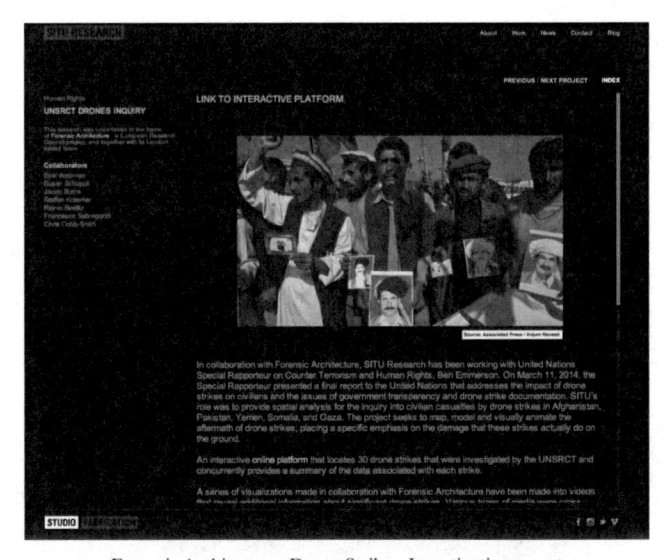

Forensic Architecture. Drone Strikes, Investigating covert
operations through spatial media

85

the idea that you're taking a large geopolitical geographic context and looking at the details. A lot of the work that's been done tends to remain at that large scale, looking at all of the FATA [Federally Administered Tribal Areas in Pakistan], or all of the casualties at once, but we want to let people look more closely.

Visual language tends to reach a broader audience, and it does make the content more accessible. Hopefully a lot of people who wouldn't otherwise be involved in the discourse will see it. We have a hope that accountability will increase as the work becomes available to a broader audience, an audience that might otherwise not read the PDF that Ben submitted at the general assembly.

Josh Begley (JB) I also enter this conversation with digital landscapes, specifically the topography of the touchscreen. I'm curious about those of us that walk down the street in an infinite scroll. What are the things that we choose to be notified about in real time? Facebook, text messages, Snapchats? I can remember this moment right after everyone joined Twitter, I was walking down Broadway, seeing folks on their phones, and I thought, "What are the landscapes these folks are least connected to?" And by "these folks" I mean me as well. What are the spaces of exception that, for all intents and purposes, could not be further away? For me, there was a grand irony to the chasm between the fetishization of the real time—the always needing to be in the loop—and the way in which war was increasingly being prosecuted overseas remotely, with many of the country's most technophiliac taxpayers completely out of the loop. These were secret wars—covert wars—that were out of sight and out of mind.

In the same way, the United States has built warehouses for people: five thousand, three hundred and ninety three carceral facilities constellating the country, many of which are constructed on far flung landscapes that, by design, are hidden from public view.

I think that there's a parallel to be drawn between the disappearing act that has been the U.S. targeted killing campaign and the landscape of the prison system. I was curious about the landscapes that I didn't have to see. A Predator drone in flight. A village in Al Jawf. The aftermath of a drone strike. A hellfire missile with "In memory of the honorable Ronald Reagan" written on the side. Nabeela, who is Mamana's granddaughter, drew her self portrait with two crayon drones circling above her house.

I was curious about my own relationship to covert war. No matter how many Amy Goodman headlines I heard about so called militants, drone strikes and aerial bombardments, I couldn't tell you in any granular detail what exactly was going on. Three thousand people died on 9/11. In the years since, as many as four thousand and seven hundred people have been killed by drones. And that's only counting the secret ones in Pakistan, Yemen, and Somalia. That's also not to say that counting isn't itself a colonial legacy.

I started with this thing that everyone has in their pocket, which is the telephone. If this is where people are, then how do you meet them there? So I decided I wanted to make an app. And I wanted to be really simple. I just wanted to send you a push notification every time a U.S. drone strike was reported in the news. In the same way that a missile can come out of nowhere, a push notification can come out of nowhere. It's not your friend texting you; it's something that's a bit more unsettling. Even if we have access to the data, do we really want to be interrupted by it? Do we really want to be as connected to our foreign policy as we are to our smartphones? Our phones, which are these increasingly intimate devices, we use them to share pictures of our loved ones and communicate with our friends. They're the things that we pull out of our pocket when we're lost, which auto-magically put us at the center of the map and tell us where we're going. Do we really want these things to also be the site of how we experience remote war? In an age when it's possible to sit in an air-conditioned room in Nevada or New Mexico and control an airplane as it hovers over a village in what used to be India. Is there a way to close that feedback loop and actually feel something, even if it's just my pocket vibrating when the missile hits the ceiling?

Dronestream. Screen Shot 2014-06-26 at 12.40.15 PM

One problem: I didn't know how to make an app. So I learned how to make an app. I submitted it to Apple and they said, "sorry, your app has been rejected." They said that it was not useful or entertaining enough, that it did not appeal to a broad enough audience. On the third rejection notice, they said that it had "excessively objectionable or crude content." This is the rationale that I got for the fourth and fifth rejections as well.

So instead I started a Twitter account, and decided to tweet the entire history of U.S. drone strikes, starting at the beginning. I said that it was going to take ten minutes, to bear witness to this on a real-time platform. It took five months. Part of the reason it took so long is because even though there have been close to five hundred reported drone strikes, there is not a lot of information. You may see a story about a strike in North Waziristan, and then see the exact same story in South Waziristan. The only thing that's different is the name of a province or the number of missiles fired. Everything else is the same. Luckily there is a fantastic organization, The Bureau of Investigative Journalism, which catalogs all of the links to these news reports.

LANDSCAPES OF SECRECY: DISCUSSION

I hope that we can get into thinking about what data means, particularly when it's human data. Particularly when it originates from wire services; when it's really just English language metadata. Basically, I went through their website, clicked on all these links, read them, tried to find some detail around which a mini-narrative could be wrapped, and then distilled it into a tweet. I also put it into a database for my graduate thesis at NYU: I made what's called an API, which is an application programming interface, so that programmers and designers can enter two lines of code and have the whole historical archive, and do something with it.

That's not to say that I don't have a critique of the fetishization of data visualizations, and our need to always show ourselves the same information over and over again. And I say that as someone who has a few different projects around drone strikes.

This is what the database looks like:

dronestream

Number	Headline	Country	Date
1	6 people killed in Marib (Marib Province)	Yemen	November 3, 2002
2	6-8 people killed in Wana (South Waziristan)	Pakistan	June 17, 2004
3	2 people killed in Toorikhel (North Waziristan)	Pakistan	May 8, 2005
4	8 people killed in Mosaki (North Waziristan)	Pakistan	November 5, 2005
5	5 people killed in Haisori (North Waziristan)	Pakistan	December 1, 2005
6	8 people killed in Saidgai (North Waziristan)	Pakistan	January 6, 2006
7	13-22 people killed in Damadola (Bajaur Agency)	Pakistan	January 13, 2006
8	81-83 people killed in Chenegai (Bajaur Agency)	Pakistan	October 30, 2006
9	8 people killed in Zamazola (South Waziristan)	Pakistan	January 16, 2007
10	3-4 people killed in Saidgai (North Waziristan)	Pakistan	April 27, 2007
11	20-34 people killed in Mami Rogha (North Waziristan)	Pakistan	June 19, 2007
12	5-10 people killed in Danda Darpakhel (North Waziristan)	Pakistan	November 2, 2007
13	Unknown people killed in Jani Khel (Bannu Frontier)	Pakistan	December 3, 2007
14	12-15 people killed in Mir Ali (North Waziristan)	Pakistan	January 29, 2008
15	8-13 people killed in Azam Warsak (South Waziristan)	Pakistan	February 28, 2008
16	12-20 people killed in Dhook Pir Bagh (South Waziristan)	Pakistan	March 16, 2008
17	12-20 people killed in Damadola (Bajaur Agency)	Pakistan	May 14, 2008
18	1 person killed in Makeen (South Waziristan)	Pakistan	June 14, 2008

Dronestream. Screen Shot 2014-06-26 at 12.33.05 PM

There's a search function, if you want to go back and actually look for a particular strike you can see the reports.

This is a thought about the notion of blank spots in the data. It's about people whose identities are not altogether known. How do you represent that information? Here, I hide each strike behind a numbered, blank tile.

I want to close with one more image, because I think that it's particularly salient for today.

If you look closely, there's a drone in flight. This is over Sana'a, where there have not been any drone strikes. As of two weeks ago, this image was still live. Anyway, that's it.

AHM We should make clear here that a lot of this reporting is done as, Josh just demonstrated, with open source information. Something like Google Earth is an incredibly powerful tool. In fact, there are some people who just spend hours and hours on Google Earth, looking for evidence of the drone program. It's kind of funny, in a sense, that data is such an issue in this time when we have access to investigative tools that are much more powerful than anything that we have had at any point in history. A lot of the statistics that I gave earlier are just collated from news reports than anyone can search for online. There are some exceptions, people who are actually in the field.

To the panelists: is there a difference for the layperson reading these reports whether there have been two thousand people killed or three thousand people killed? Or is the real change going to happen through developing these narratives? Does it really matter that we don't have access to perfect information about drone strikes?

NS Well, I'm of two minds. I'm a lobbyist for the ACLU, so I'm in the business of trying to get the U.S. government to change its policies of surveilling, detaining and killing people.

In trying to make the case to the government, it is of foremost importance to be able to show that people like you guys actually care. For Amnesty, we made a conscious choice to focus on the killing of a grandmother and the killing of a fourteen-year-old boy. By focusing on those stories instead of the big numbers, we were able to break through the media conversation, and as a result we got far more media coverage than we had anticipated. It was an unprecedented level of media coverage for Amnesty worldwide. I think it was because of that message, a grandmother. It's an indisputable message.

When you can't put the faces by the numbers, these statistics play into the presumptions that we have about who lives in those places. If you even look at the language of the media reports, like the CNN reports, the terms used are "compounds," "vehicles," "militants," "North Waziristan," which sounds like "warrior." It's difficult for people in the United States or people in the United Kingdom to really grasp those terms. But when you describe a grandmother dying while her grandkids are watching, that really gets to people.

On the other hand, if you take the case to a member of Congress or to the White House and say, "look you killed this grandmother," they say, "okay even if we did, we're also killing thousands of bad guys."

But even then, the words "militants" and "bad guys" are completely meaningless. These vaguely legal terms end up obscuring the urgency of finding out these peoples' identities. For the administration and for the members of Congress, the issue really is "Who are the thousands of people who have been killed?" If we can show that thousands of people have been killed illegally then that might change the way this Congress thinks about the issue. Currently, the numbers they do have are from the CIA, and so they have those numbers against Amnesty's numbers, or Amnesty's one grandmother.

AHM Brad, are the visual reconstructions of each strike site an attempt to enrich the data somehow—to make it more valuable to the researcher—or is it a way of making it more accessible to the public?

BS There are two ways to answer. Given that this is a covert program in a very remote part of the world, we often resign ourselves to the fact that we can only know very little. Whether it's willful or just passive, that resignation results in a certain type of complicity. It's too early for us to say what the efficacy of the work is, but by doing this work, by cross-referencing to find the exact location of a strike, for example, we can begin to get more and more specific. In addition, there's an analytical potential for how to use spatial information, which we're trying to leverage. On the most basic level, it's about demonstrating that there is the potential to know more, yes, while at the same time reaching a broader audience. Some of the more involved digital modeling and satellite analysis begins to be more analytical as well.

> **AHM** Perhaps there's a tension here between two of the methodologies. Brad's work is about attracting people to the data by demonstrating that it isn't as impenetrable as we think. Josh is looking to interrupt our lives. He is saying, "No, can't be indifferent." He is bringing the data into our own pockets. Is there a tension between those two methodologies?

JB I made the app because I didn't think anyone would want to download it. I didn't think people really want to subscribe to these alerts. I also started the Twitter account because I didn't think anyone would want to follow it. People believe that if you have access to the facts the data will set you free; I think that is false. I think that the way that we make sense of the world is through narrative. And so, in some ways, I've been playing in this space of meta-narrative, where the narrative is the counting. I guess the purpose of counting these things on the Internet is to show that I actually can't count them. I'm not sure what that means, but when I hear "two thousand" or when I hear "three thousand" or when I hear "five thousand," it doesn't do much for me. But when I hear somebody speak about his lived experience, it does.

BS We're perhaps, hopefully, departing from the period of fetishization of the quantitative. Human Rights Watch hired its first statistician a few years ago. That says something about the direction we're heading, but I think the point is that the disciplines tend to be siloed. And so the goal is to be able to bring the narrative in, because it enriches our understanding of what occurred and because it allows us to leverage the data and to refuse to be in these silos.

AHM And Naureen, where do you think an organization like Amnesty International stands in that tension?

NS We're desperate to get things to change, and both of these efforts are incredibly important. I was just thinking about Senator Dianne Feinstein from California. She is one of the most important people on this issue—she's the Chair of the Select Committee on Intelligence—and she revealed a couple of weeks ago at a congressional hearing about domestic drones that she wanted the technology to be regulated because she recently saw a drone outside of her window and it really bothered her. This is so painful, considering the drones that, under her watch, are not only outside peoples' windows but are destroying those peoples' homes and their families. That data and that narrative serve to disrupt and obstruct the cheerful narrative about killing the terrorists.

That being said, we can't have just the stories like the testimony that I read you. They don't really go far enough, because ultimately policy-makers have bigger questions. For that, I think the biggest problem is that Amnesty couldn't get behind what the Bureau of Investigative Journalism is doing because we can't interrogate all of that data. We can't put forward anything unless we are quite sure that it really did happen. The reports the news stories are so flawed; they're relying on Pakistani military officials to confirm the number of people killed. They're relying on local witnesses who might have been intimidated by the Taliban or by other armed groups. We're talking about a part of the world where the U.S. presence is incredibly politicized; people are really angry about it for a lot of different reasons and there's a huge amount of propaganda about the U.S. killing. The high court of Peshawar in Pakistan handed down a decision that claims the vast majority of the drone strikes have killed mothers and suckling babies. So there's hyperbole that goes far beyond what is often the case. We just have to be really, really careful with the data, which is why I think it's so important what both Josh and Brad have been doing.

AHM People talk about the drone strike program as being a "secret program," and yet we actually know a great deal about it. While we may not have perfectly accurate information, we know that people are killed; know that buildings are destroyed and we know that sometimes civilians die. The whole idea of secrecy is, perhaps, really just a fallacy. What, then, is the actual benefit of having the government give us exact numbers?

NS It goes to the theory of change. If you don't have accountability for human rights violations, you can expect the perpetrators to continue to conduct them. A few weeks ago, the Senate voted to declassify a report on the torture of people that occurred under the Bush administration. We know that hundreds of people were tortured, that the CIA destroyed the tapes that they had made of them torturing people, and then we have that same agency that is put in charge of killing people globally outside of public view. Then we have that same intelligence community that is in charge of surveilling people around the world and has unprecedented access to every single persons phone, computer, this room right now. Obviously, we know that surveillance and torture and killing have happened, but secrecy is a stand-in for obstructing accountability. No one at the

LANDSCAPES OF SECRECY: DISCUSSION

CIA ever had to pay for what happened. If you were a part of the CIA, and you had never been held to account for your actions, why wouldn't you think that you could just keep on doing it? They continue to commit abuses with impunity—it's a word that we use a lot. Impunity happens because we never stop and force them to admit that they actually did the deed. They never take any kind of punishment, even from the public, and it just keeps on going and it's almost like Whack-a-Mole for the human rights advocates. So, an end to the secrecy would be a start to accountability.

AHM Josh, Brad, do your feelings about the policy interfere with, or influence, your methodologies?

JB I'm interested in definitions of secrecy that are not reduced to simply what you do or don't get to know. I'm looking for definitions that have more of a material element to them. One of the reasons I love Trevor Paglen's work is that he takes seriously the idea of secrecy being a material reality that is sculpted by human beings. By looking at buildings and infrastructure, we can see the places that the invisible world intersects the visible world.

There are news reports about drone strikes that say forty-two people were sitting outside of a bus depot when a missile struck, and that same year John Brennan, the director of the CIA, says that there has not been a single civilian casualty. That is also one of those places that the visible and the invisible intersect. I am drawn to the project, in some ways, because of that. Do my opinions get in the way? Well, I'm trying to just make sense of it for myself, and chart a kind of geography for this program. This is more than just putting the place marks on the map. In order to think about where these strikes take place, you have to develop an understanding of the political geography of Yemen or of FATA. Before I started the project, I just hadn't really looked in a very granular way at the map of Yemen, and so by simply learning the names of different provinces, one can make the whole geography of secrecy a little bit less secret.

That may not be getting to your point. When I started tweeting the drone strikes, I used the word "civilian." And about halfway through I realized that I wasn't not really sure what I meant by that word, and likewise what I didn't meant by it. The word implies something about all these people whom I don't actually know anything about.

AHM A couple of years ago it was revealed that in the United States government's tallies any military aged male killed in the vicinity of a drone strike is not counted as a civilian. He's counted as a "combatant." You're right, Josh, that the question of being a civilian or not is very, very complicated.

Brad, what do you want to see happen with the platform now? Is it to become an archival piece that you want people to keep returning to, or will it continue to develop?

> **BS** Accountability in general begins to structure behavior. Our ambition with this platform is to increase transparency and accountability. So it doesn't stop with the report; it's built in a way that allows any and all commissions to be updated. We'll see how effective it is. I don't even really think we're talking about drones, actually. We're talking about extrajudicial killing and we're talking about territoriality, we're talking about international law. The technology will come and go. This technology has forced a debate and discourse around certain issues that are really important.

Question from the audience (QFA) *Naureen, can you speak a little bit to the basic legality or illegality of these U.S. drone strikes?*

> **NS** There is international human rights law and then there are the laws of war that apply only in situations of armed conflict. There's an armed conflict that's happening in Afghanistan. But in Pakistan, is it an armed conflict?

The U.S. would say that, yes, there is an armed conflict in Pakistan. It would say that we are in a global armed conflict with al Qaeda and its associated forces. That global armed conflict is boundless in territory—it could be anywhere—and it is boundless in time. It is going to continue indefinitely. According to the Obama Administration's theory of armed conflict, everyone is either a civilian or a combatant. If you are a combatant, you can be directly targeted. And if I'm a particularly significant combatant—say, Osama Bin Laden—it might be lawful for the civilians around me to be killed, if that's what it will take to kill me too, because they can be considered collateral damage.

The answer to the question first depends first on whether you are in an armed conflict, but second of all depends on the idea of an imminent threat. Under international human rights law, you can only use lethal force under a truly imminent threat where there is no other alternative, where it is a last resort. The question in these cases, why it's not simple, why Ben Emmerson's report doesn't simply say in these thirty cases there was an unlawful killing, is because these inquiries are very fact dependent. The underlying issue is that the onus is on the United States to establish the legality of any of these strikes. When Ben Emmerson puts forward thirty cases or when Ben Emmerson puts forward nine, the administration has an obligation under international law to investigate these allegations and to provide information about them, and the administration has failed on both counts, and in that way I personally think they have violated international law.

QFA *I am wondering if there are any other countries that have started to develop the same technologies, or if they have begun to enter the dispute between other countries over these technologies.*

> **AHM** It might come as a bit of a surprise, but there are about one hundred countries around the world that are developing drones.

It is a question that is very much tied up in the issue of access to satellite infrastructures. Because while it may not be too difficult to build an unmanned flying vehicle, the communications systems that are necessary to enable to kind of targeted killing flights that the U.S. conducts—with pilots in Nevada controlling drones flying over Pakistan— are extremely complex and require a lot of technology that very few countries have access to.

There are also a whole number of interesting questions around the different countries that the U.S. relies on to physically carry out its targeted killing operations. Recently, a former drone pilot by the name of Brandon Bryant came out and announced that the U.S. has been using its Ramstein Air Base in Germany as a waypoint for the data passing between pilots in the U.S. and the drones flying over Somalia, Yemen and Pakistan. Does that make Germany an accessory to U.S. operations? Does that violate German democratic policy, which is for the most part opposed to the targeted killing regime? It certainly wasn't decided upon in a referendum.

This is a very complex issue, and I urge everyone to think about the role of the largely invisible infrastructures that enable drone warfare.

QFA *Is there a danger of hyper-visibility of data and can its tendency to produce certain forms of knowledge also validate the destruction of lives?*

BS It's an excellent point. The premise, for now, is that we need to create a vehicle for the flow of information. The foundation for the whole project—what we're trying to do right now—is to make as much available as possible, to get the different types of visual information to talk to each other, and to allow users to cross-reference materials. At this point, achieving that has been our main goal. We haven't given much thought to the negative consequences

JB I think the future of these sorts of drones are solar-powered drones that can be hanging up there for a year or two and will have a very high-resolution camera on them, that can watch over an entire medium-sized city and go back in time and look and identify the various hyper-visible disposable bodies. Facebook announced that it plans to do the same sort of thing. They said they are going to be able to beam network access to places that don't have Internet, with drones that are going to be at sixty-five-thousand feet because it's above the legislative airspace. I imagine that there will be a nexus between giving people Internet—"connecting the world"—and having a camera that can be accessed by law enforcement. Those two things will intersect in an interesting way.

AHM Let's just take one more.

QFA *Is there a special sauce with regards to both policy-making and design in creating these modes of information to display and share with lawmakers and policy-makers? Where do you see the barriers that otherwise keep that from happening?*

BS It's on the designer to approach the policy-makers, the people working in human rights, the lawyers. These key players are, in my experience, really receptive to this kind of work but just wouldn't know to ask for it, much less use it. They wouldn't necessarily know how to use modeling software, or be able to decide which remote-sensing data to use. But to go in and make a presentation to Human Rights Watch or to make a presentation somewhere and show them what can be done, then you initiate the long process.

For example, the Human Right Watch approached us and said "we're working on a case in Syria, and it would be great if you could help us out—we want to show how many bodies fit in detention centers of different sizes." The designer can start the conversation that otherwise might not happen. In my experience, that's how things get started.

AHM We're at the end of the first decade of drone use. What happens in the next decade is probably going to be even more incredible and transformative and challenging. Much depends, I think, on the public being informed. The three people you have in front of you are at the forefront of informing the public. And while, yes, we can read the human rights reports and navigate through Dronestream and the SITU platform, we also have to actively seek out and demand better data ourselves.

This event transcript was edited and condensed

THE DRONE SALON

The Drone Salon

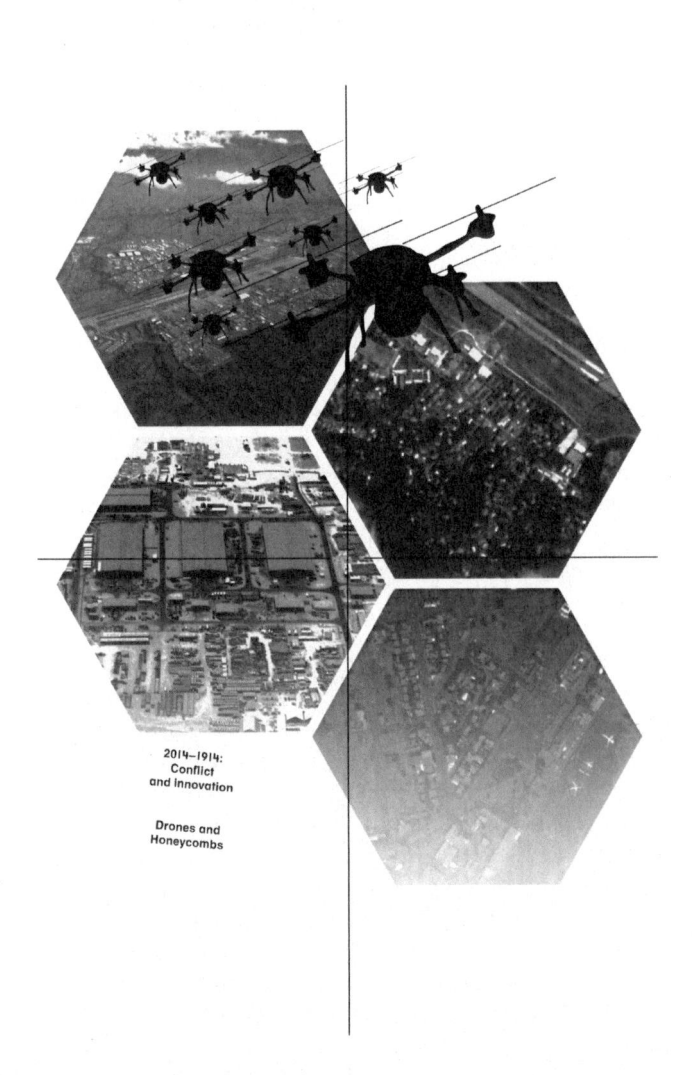

2014–1914:
Conflict
and innovation

Drones and
Honeycombs

UNMANNED   ARCHITECTURE AND SECURITY SERIES

A New View from Above, a Report on the Drone Salon
Jane Szita

May 23, 2014
Het Nieuwe Instituut, Rotterdam

There have been other events devoted to the contemporary phenomenon of drones, but none has called itself a "salon" before. A gleeful Guus Beumer, director of Rotterdam's Het Nieuwe Instituut, which hosted the event, revealed in its title, with its "unlikely pairing" of associations and expectations. Drones, the potentially deadly airborne robots, would seem to have little to do with "the salon", that refined type of gathering invented by the enlightenment to further Horace's aims of poetry, "either to please or to educate."

But Beumer directed our attention to a previous FAST— the Foundation for Achieving Seamless Territory— event, staged at the Marres Centre in Maastricht, which framed the desperate situation in Gaza in the context of the zoo, refreshing the issue with an angle as much popular and poetic as it was polemic—and thus enabling "another kind of discussion" entirely. Similarly, FAST's Drone Salon, a collaboration with dpr-barcelona, set out to reinvigorate a topic all too often rendered two-dimensional by rhetoric, hysteria and hype— whether applied to the drone's military incarnation as a rapidly escalating but largely opaque weapon in conflicts in Pakistan and Yemen, or to the business ambitions of Amazon, promising, in the next half-decade, "Prime Air" delivery via drone within thirty minutes.

A NEW VIEW FROM ABOVE

Drones have exploded in more ways than one into the unprepared world of the twenty-first century. The market as estimated by the drone industry itself (in the shape of the Association for Unmanned Vehicle Systems International) will be worth an estimated eighty-two billion dollars by 2025, while employing one hundred thousand people. Behind this expansion, agencies from civil aviation authorities to international lawyers grapple with drone implications, legal and otherwise. The Salon, in two parts, set out to examine not only these issues, but their wider ripples in the cultural landscape; the drone's manifestations in conflicts, but also in civilian, built and social urban space.

Warfare and the City

As director of FAST and initiator of the event, Malkit Shoshan spoke first, explaining the wider context of the Salon as part of a tripartite examination of architecture in contemporary conflict covering missions, compounds and drones.

Drones, Shoshan pointed out, have taken conflicts away from the battleground and into an altogether more ambiguous space. "In the contemporary organization of conflict, the old notion of war and peace no longer exists as a spatial division," she said. "War takes place in civic space—and it therefore necessitates the military to update its warfare doctrine."

Drone Salon. Event impression

Hence the new rhetoric of counterinsurgency, which aims to identify the terrorists hiding among civilians: "Soldiers therefore need to observe civic space, how people move through it and use it, listing individuals and mapping their movements. These observations turned into data that was used to create a dynamic matrix, to evaluate threat. By now the distinction of threat is no longer based on proof, but on probability."

"The warfare strategy that was used in Afghanistan turned to be the most expensive mission in history," continued Shoshan. "It was difficult to sell the costs at home. A better solution had to be found." Drones—controlled from afar, and given a pre-set mission—were the answer: reducing, or at least appearing to reduce, costs and casualties, they also transformed the way conflicts are seen not only by observers, but also participants. "Drones make us see our environment as never before—their sensors and cameras see objects not visible to the human eye."

But perhaps, in line with the new objective of removing every threat, they also make us see what is not there, as was suggested by a White House bureaucrat anonymously quoted in *The New York Times* and cited by Shoshan:

> "The joke was that when the CIA sees 'three guys doing jumping jacks,' the agency thinks it is a terrorist training camp, said one senior official."

From this drone operator's eye view, Shoshan then zoomed in on those under CIA scrutiny, citing the testimony of Pakistani women living under the daily reality of drone patrols. "After the first attacks, they retreated from markets and cultural facilities; and after a drone hits the school, they stopped their kids going there. But then, drones start to target homes." This unprecedented step effects "a fundamental ethical transformation regarding civic space. Architecture is a sense of comfort and safety. It houses our social networks. Attacking civic society and turning it into the front line is relevant to us all."

This, she concluded, is the essential point needing to be addressed by the Salon and by two further projects that will follow on from it. *Retreat*, a collaborative design and research project, will explore the option of withdrawal, while *Unmanned* will be a public project on the spatial and ethical impact of drones.

Ravens to Reapers

The next presentation gave the audience an up-close view of the drone—or to use the preferred NATO terminology, the Unmanned Aerial System (UAS)—in the Dutch military context, courtesy of Lieutenant-colonel Pieter Mink, who is a senior advisor in UAS for the Royal Netherlands Army Command.

> "The Dutch armed forces do not have and will not have armed drones—we use them only for intelligence gathering," Mink stated. The Netherlands currently has two systems operational on land and sea; one of their most important uses is to support "national operations—the police, fire service, local government."

A quick scan of the different drones available showed a range from the micro drone—an insect-like concoction weighing a few grams and suited for built-up areas—and the toy-scale

Lieutenant-colonel Pieter Mink, the Royal Netherlands Army Command

A presentation by Belkis Wille via Skype. A Human Rights Watch representative in Sana, Yemen

mini drone, right up to the top of the pyramid where we find the Global Hawk, with a wingspan of almost forty meters, rising up to twenty thousand meters in altitude and with an endurance of forty-eight hours, far beyond that of a manned aircraft.

The Lieutenant-colonel stressed that the UAS is a system, consisting not only of the air vehicle but also a Ground Control Station (GCS), plus an operator or operators. Dutch forces currently have twenty-four of these systems, divided between the Raven and Scan Eagle, but there are also plans to acquire two new types. Meanwhile, the Raven with its 1.4 meter wingspan can be launched by hand and is viewed as a set of "flying binoculars," providing "more situational awareness for soldiers on the ground."

The Scan Eagle, with a wider 3.1 meter wingspan and higher endurance, is a dual operator system—the flight operator is joined by the "payload operator" for the camera. Used onboard the HNLMS Rotterdam, the Scan Eagle has been used successfully in Somalia, where it reduced piracy by revealing the "complete logistics chain of the pirates" after long periods of surveillance.

Videos showed the drones in use, the Scan Eagle at sea and the Raven launched by hand during a reconnaissance patrol in South Africa, then streaming aerial images to a laptop for analysis. Subsequent footage showed many civilian-context uses of drones by the Dutch police force and fire and other state departments, including the usage of a drone to locate a suspect and make an arrest; to monitor the New Year riots at Veen; to detect cannabis farms and illegal hunting; to inspect the country's dehydrated peat dykes; to investigate dune fires; and for surveillance during the NATO summit.

"You are Scared of not Being Under a Roof"

According to the Bureau of Investigative Journalism, there have been around sixty-four to seventy-six confirmed U.S. drone strikes in Yemen since 2004. Human Rights Watch's Belkis Wille joined the Salon via Skype to report from Yemen, where, she said, "it would be unrealistic to say there isn't a war in the south".

Being based in Sana'a, Wille does not currently live under the perpetual hum of drones: "We currently have few drone attacks here—there have been periods of greater activity." From Southern Yemen, however, she reports there are continual complaints about "the constant noise, and the feeling of being watched. Also, as a Yemeni, you feel that your national sovereignty is being undermined and that you are monitored by foreign governments. It really increases anti-American sentiment, although the U.S. Defense Department always says that the Western media plays it up, and Yemenis aren't really concerned with drone strikes.

> "At Human Rights Watch, we frequently release reports," Wille continued. "At six recent press conferences for these, of which five had nothing to do with drone strikes, the first question was always: 'Why aren't you doing more about drone strikes?' That issue is top of the list for Yemenis."

The Human Rights Watch position on drones is that "not all drone strikes are wrong—our position is that there are cases in which drone strikes are lawful and others in which they are unlawful. To be lawful, they must minimize civilian casualties."

"In Yemen, the problem is that because the U.S. is covertly carrying out drone strikes, it does not do what it did in Afghanistan and Iraq—namely, issue a statement naming the target and civilian casualties. Also, it has no compensation scheme as it did in Iraq. This absence of a statement backfires on a policy level, as terrorists can claim all casualties are civilian. In my experience, however, there are low numbers of civilian casualties."

Nevertheless, "anger is disproportionate. If there is a drone strike, there is a demand for information. Under the laws of war, taking out a couple of civilians with a legitimate target is considered OK. But the problem here is, we can conclude that maybe two out of six strikes are unlawful—but it's hard to say. When a wedding convoy is attacked—is that lawful? We don't have the information, so we can't say. We put the responsibility squarely on the U.S., although the Yemeni government is complicit and gives permission. The Yemeni government compensates only powerful tribes."

Human Rights Watch, Wille reported, is now working with Yemenis on making demands—including for a compensation scheme like that in Afghanistan or Iraq. Meanwhile life in Yemen is changing, she said: "Do drones change the way cities are used? It's only anecdotal evidence I have, but yes they do—they led

Conversation between Quirine Eijkman, A representative of Amnesty International, Malkit Shoshan (FAST) and Catherine Harwood, an international law researcher (Leiden University)

people to avoid being outdoors in Sana'a when there were strikes here. I hear from others that 'drones shut you in, because you are scared of being not under a roof.'"

"Will I be Next?"

The following presentation, by Amnesty International's Quirine Eijkman, took us to another region targeted by armed drones, and to the research of Amnesty International, namely its report entitled *Will I Be Next?*. "This may surprise you, but at Amnesty we don't take issue with drones as such. However, some examples of U.S. strikes in Pakistan may violate international law," she said. "Nine out of forty-five strikes between January 2012 and August 2013 on the border of Pakistan and Afghanistan are under question."

Eijkman stressed the great difficulty of establishing the facts on the ground, echoing what we had just learned about the lack of transparency in Yemen: "People who talk to us for research take a high personal risk—some are visited by security forces. There are significant international legal challenges, but what we want is more accountability and transparency."

In the face of the covert nature of drone attacks in the Federally Administered Tribal Areas (FATA) in North Waziristan, a heavily contested region, gathering information is challenging: satellite images must be used to establish the sites of strikes. Nevertheless, Eijkman was able to list the particulars of one, presumably unlawful strike in all its tragic detail. The sixty-year-old grandmother Mamana Bibi was killed October 24, 2012, as she worked in her family's fields with her grandchildren—some of whom were hurt in a second strike, which caused nine serious injuries.

> "The total lack of accountability means there has been no investigation or compensation," said Eijkman. "Was Mamana Bibi perceived as a threat? Was she a target, or was this a 'signature' strike [the term given to strikes against individuals who match a pre-identified 'signature'

UNMANNED ARCHITECTURE AND SECURITY SERIES

of behavior that the U.S. links to militant activity]? What is the legal basis? Lack of transparency makes it impossible to assess. Was it a war crime, or an extra-judicial execution?"

Amnesty questions the fact that under such circumstances there is no justice for victims, who cannot get compensation—in this case, the victims' family had to sell part of their land so that the children could receive medical treatment. "In mid-May 2013, Obama promised more transparency," said Eijkman. "But this has not happened. One of Mamana's grandchildren went to the U.S. congress to tell her story, but only four members were present to listen to her."

Toxic Roads

For Eyal Weizman, who then addressed the Salon via Skype, "being remotely present is like a drone-operated lecture." Weizman, professor of visual cultures and director of the Centre for Research Architecture at Goldsmiths, University of London, is also director of the European Research Council-funded project, Forensic Architecture, on the place of architecture in international humanitarian law.

Forensic Architecture "assumes we are in a time when war has important urban dimensions," Weizman said. "Drones are assumed to operate in remote areas, but they are largely used in

Eyal Weizman presentation on Forensic Architecture

densely populated urban and rural environments. War has moved into the city. Forensic Architecture is an attempt to understand conflict through the built environment. Urban analysis can teach us something about the people being killed."

A report by Forensic Architecture therefore looks at different target types—the places hit, and number of casualties of drone strikes:

> "For the first time, public places are being struck, public or private buildings," said Weizman. "I am interested in what the patterns of buildings hit can tell us about war. How does it affect our interpretation of a conflict? Signature strikes target people through 'suspicious' patterns of behavior, including movement along so-called 'toxic' roads. People on the ground are being hunted."

Following a drone strike, people act differently, avoiding roads and taking covered routes, "so there is a constant co-evolution between the pattern or algorithm and people's behavior. Living under drones is not static. It's a pattern of co-learning, between the ground and air." Studying these shifting patterns reveals that not only people and algorithms are dynamic, but so is the legal framework. Just as people's behavior is changed by algorithms and strikes (and vice versa), so rhetoric changes perceptions and legal attitudes: "What is happening now is attempted legislation. When Israel started targeted assassinations, these were at first not accepted as legal. But Israel kept doing it and offering its own interpretations, and they are now more or less accepted. So we need to act not only on behalf of the victims, but also of international law. The law has a degree of elasticity—and states want to shift it to their advantage."

International Law: Horizontal, with an Enforcement Problem

The following presentation, by researcher Catharine Harwood of the University of Haarlem, the Netherlands, focused on international law, which, she explained, is still attempting to get to grips with the "recent phenomenon" of armed drones.

UNMANNED ARCHITECTURE AND SECURITY SERIES

Catherine Harwood, an international law researcher at Leiden University

"The only states in world to use armed drones so far are the U.S., UK and Israel—also apparently the non-state actor Hezbollah," Harwood said. "They are not prohibited under international law," but their legality "depends on the context."

International law, in any case, is a problematic and often hazy concept: "All states have a duty to respect international law, but it is a horizontal system, with an enforcement problem: the laws apply to the very states which make them and enforce them."

The situation with drones is compounded because international humanitarian law applies only in international armed conflicts, and not to the war on terror in which drones are largely used. Furthermore, "The U.S. and Israel don't accept that human rights apply in armed conflict, although otherwise that is generally accepted."

International conflict is defined as occurring between states, and soldiers are 'combatants'; non-international armed conflict occurs between groups, or states and groups, and there is no combatant status, with "a certain spillover of non-international conflict tolerated, but the question remains as to how great this may be." A new category, trans-national war, is not legally recognized but refers to conflicts crossing borders with non-state actors.

In non-international armed conflicts, "civilians can be targeted, it depends on what they are doing." In fact, under international law, attacks on civilians are technically "limited to organized armed groups and civilians directly participating in hostilities—there are strict criteria. One big problem in practice are signature strikes. The U.S. targets people based on location, age and the fact of being male—so this is quite concerning."

In the Netherlands, how Many Terrorists Would the Algorithm Find?

A short discussion concluded this first part of the program, during which the lack of transparency regarding drones emerged as the most striking feature of the new landscape, said Malkit Shoshan: "Everything is blurring. Many different zones overlap with each other. I started looking at drones after researching the architecture of peace-keeping missions—drones change combat, but also the way the military is operating so it can be more involved in aid, redevelopment and organizing civic space."

Quirine Eijkman countered Pieter Mink's emphatic statement that the Dutch army has no plans to use armed drones by pointing out that the new drones it plans to buy have the potential to be armed. "The issue with drones is when non-armed drone nations share information with different agencies," Eijkman added. "This leads to complications. The Dutch have shared information collected by drone in Mali with other nations. Legally, this is unclear. It's a big issue in the EU, because European partners share information about Yemen and Pakistan with the U.S."

Catherine Harwood stressed that, "with drones, some functions are benign. Others are not. There's a need for information and transparency. In March, the UN voted on greater transparency in drone use, and six states voted against that. So we need to insist on it."

> "Intervening before an act takes place does not preclude some information on the legitimacy of targets," added Eijkman. "We should be able to question what the indicators are." Harwood stated that "People involved in targeting have to have responsibility—if a machine does it, people will no longer be criminally responsible."

At this point a member of the audience suggested a way of making people more aware of algorithms. "If we applied the algorithm to the Netherlands, how many terrorists would we find?" he asked. Although the Salon was felt to be a step in the right direction, policy-makers, it seemed, could try harder. "Politicians are interested only in how safe drones are, and rules of privacy," observed Pieter Mink.

Ethel Baraona Pohl presents 'From the battlefield to Adhocracy'

A NEW VIEW FROM ABOVE

From the Battlefield to Adhocracy

"I am looking for you like a drone, my love. You have become Osama, no one knows your whereabouts."

A Pakistani folk poem kicked-off the presentation of Ethel Baraona Pohl and began the second part of the program, with a focus on cultural and societal enquiry. Baraona Pohl paraphrased Cedric Price to ask us: "Drones are the answer, but what was the question?" Despite a range of real and potential applications, from anti-wildlife poaching to pizza delivery, the answer is unclear. Legally, too, drones inhabit a twilight zone:

> "You can buy a drone in a toy store, and they're all over YouTube, but U.S. law still doesn't know what to do with them."
> —Aviva Rutkin in *New Scientist*

Despite the confusion, drones are not a new invention. Nicholas Tesla pioneered the concept one hundred years ago. The army began to adopt them after the Second World War, with the Ryan models of the 1950s being the prototypes of today's drones. Baraona Pohl argued that the sudden take-off of drones in the last ten years may have much to do with cultural factors, ranging from Kathleen Ann Goonan's 1994 sci-fi novel *Queen City Jazz* to Wikileaks footage.

Beyond war, drones feature in advertising, agriculture, journalism, wildlife conservation and real-estate marketing. They can be used by activists as well as the establishment.

Baraona Pohl's presentation quickly surveyed El Salvador's drone journalism, and art projects such as James Bridle's *Dronestagram* and the Metadata+ app by Josh Begley, both of which document drone strikes as they happen. Bridle's *Drone Shadow* paintings make visible the usually unseen, while the large-scale close-ups of #notabugsplat.com are designed to confront drone operators with the human faces they normally do not have to see. The presentation ended with another piece of Pakistani folk poetry:

> "Your eyes are no less than a drone. They turned me into ashes as I was facing them, like a member of the Taliban."

When Drones are Democratized

"Drones are not objects but systems," Liam Young reminded us in the following presentation, "although we fetishize them as objects." Young, founder of the think-tank, Tomorrow's Thoughts Today, is an architect who believes that "the physical city is dissolving, its social structures like squares giving way to nomadic ones like networks and algorithms."

Drones "allow us to collapse geographies. The drone network is a form of teleportation—a drone station in Australia coordinates strikes in the Middle East." The drone infrastructure represents weaponized connectivity, so Young's organization has responded with a concept called *Silent Protest*: "Gliders in fleets surf air currents, generate white noise and temporarily jam telecom infrastructures."

Such initiatives may seem far-fetched, but are becoming increasingly plausible. "Civilian drones now outnumber military

Liam Young presents 'Drones and the Collapse of Geographies'

ones," said Young. "We are on the edge of imagining what they might be deployed for. It's like the dawn of the PC. When drones are democratized, what will happen next?" He envisages "flocks of drones like an airborne Napster or Pirate Bay—people could log on to file-share. It's a new form of nomadic infrastructure. Drones might generate geographically specific technological neighborhoods."

Taking as a starting point Los Angeles' hidden landscape of helipads—every building over twenty meters high is apparently equipped with one—, Young speculated that "landing pads for drones might shape our city. And cities: how will they change so that drones can navigate them?" He predicted the evolution of "a new visual language based on calibration graffiti—this could also be subversive, causing surveillance drones to crash into walls."

In this new infrastructure of the sky, Young asked, "will Amazon drones herald a new gold rush? Will drones become so ubiquitous they start to disappear in our consciousness like pigeons? The buzz of the drone is the sound of our generation. A bottom-up technology will reveal itself. Pushing against authority, democratization will make it clear what drones can do."

Ruben Paters presents the Drone Survival Guide

Drone Survivalism

Dutch artist Ruben Pater sees drones as defining "a new habitat"—there are, he said, thirty thousand of them predicted to shortly occupy the U.S., after all. Just as our remote ancestors could recognize the silhouettes of dangerous birds of prey as they soared above the ground, Pater imagines a day—already here for some—when we will distinguish between threatening and harmless drones in the sky. This idea informed his *Drone Survival Guide*, a drone-spotter's collection of the most common "species," illustrated according to scale, from the Parrot drone on sale at Amazon to the huge Global Hawk currently used only by the U.S. and Germany.

The guide to drone types is accompanied by countermeasures, including hacking drones and hiding from them—seemingly, a simple survival blanket will suffice. The *Drone Survival Guide* was initially translated into Pashto, the language spoken around the lately drone-patrolled Afghanistan and Pakistan border; twenty-eight other language versions followed, all compiled by volunteers—in a clear indication of the interest in the project. "Drones are a sophisticated mirror," said Pater. "Through them we are looking at others, and at ourselves."

Decolonized Skies

Art curator Yael Messer of High&Low Bureau, working on an exhibition of drone-related art for the Apex Gallery in New York, is currently in a process she calls "a new search for ethics and aesthetics." Ruben Pater's *Drone Survival Guide* and Eyal Weizman's Forensic Architecture will be part of the show.

> "The view from above has always been a method of control used by states and other bodies to monitor situations," Messer said. "Drones involve the framing of humans in ways to justify their elimination." Art's response to this fact "offers ways to be subversive by taking control of the manipulation of images," so regaining the initiative and "decolonizing the skies".

A NEW VIEW FROM ABOVE

Yael Messer presents 'Decolonized Skies'

Matthew Stadler presents 'Drones: Angels or Demons'

Messer referenced the July 2013 action of actor George Clooney, who spent his earnings for the Nespresso campaign on a spy satellite aimed over North and South Sudan, monitoring the Sudanese dictator Omar al-Bashir—a blurring of lines between military surveillance technology and private activism.

The forthcoming *Decolonized Skies* exhibition sets out to explores the ethical, social and spatial implications of the "democratization of the view from above" through the strategies of artists such as Bik van der Pol, who "explores the layers of urban environment" in a manner that reclaims map-making from the forces of control, "empowering prospects for art and society in this time of vast change in our point of view."

Drones, Angels, Demons

"No system is unmanned; we are talking about a system that is human," said author Matthew Stadler, currently working on a novel about drones, at the outset of his presentation. A backdrop of harrowing images of small children killed by drones illuminated his use of these terms. As Stadler insisted, drones represent "a loss of moral capacity rather than an enemy we have to defeat."

YouTube images indeed revealed "a system that hasn't moved out of human realm, an HD camera on a 3D axis," an instrument of "self-regard and self-policing." Not for the first time during the Salon, the drone was revealed to be a mirror, reflecting ourselves as well as our society.

Stadler drew a parallel between the ambiguities surrounding the drone—both weapon of death and fun selfie generator—with the ambiguities of another era, the starting point of Humanism during the Renaissance. "Artists have long dealt with the problem of angels versus demons", he said, showing images of Pieter Brueghel's *The Fall of the Rebel Angels* and similar works. It is, Stadler concluded from these, "hard to tell angels and demons apart."

Art—whether Renaissance paintings and engravings or the novel Stadler is writing—is "a mode to live within a paradox;

Drone Salon. A final presentation from war to the city

to feel empathy as well as revulsion." As such, it can capture the moral ambiguity of the drone, of an age in which Stadler likens us to the clergy feasting in the mouth of the devil in a sixteenth-century woodcut. "I want to give us hope and ambition to deal with the challenge we face," he said, as Jonathan Richman's *Angels Watching Over Me* played over a slideshow of drone images. "After all, it is no greater than that at any time during the past one thousand years."

A Multi-Faceted Reality

In the closing discussion that followed, an audience member commented that the cultural speakers tended to relate the drone to the past, but doubted whether the law and military saw this continuity. Matthew Stadler argued that, "it is in the interests of the process in charge of drones to divorce them from history—the appearance of discontinuity is a deliberate political strategy. As artists and researchers, we poke holes in this."

"There is less clarity because the battlefield has changed," added Malkit Shoshan. "Drones operate in a gap, the civil space; the same forces of control now shift into big transitions we don't understand." Catherine Harwood agreed that "the need to constrain power within acceptable limits" was the thread of continuity, even if "the law is always behind technical developments."

This comment produced another remark from the audience—that in Spain a law is currently being drafted to ensure that drones cannot fly without the permission of the authorities. In the Netherlands, another audience member responded, you have to obtain prior permission six weeks in advance in order to fly anything—and, Pieter Mink added, a drone operator needs a pilot's license in the Netherlands, which is the only country to require this.

"Our capacity to invent things is much faster than our capacity to decide what they mean," pointed out Liam Young. "Our projects are about increasing visibility and awareness. This instigates cultural change. All it will take is for someone to monetize the low-flying drone and the laws will change."

Shoshan pointed out that the discussion often seemed to be about "good or bad. We are in the middle of a change. It's hard to say whether that's OK or not OK. Drones may prevent crime—but what price do we pay for that? We need the bigger picture." This is where art comes in, said Harwood: "Art can make issues more human than law. It triggers the imagination, gets you thinking in new way—and that's good for a lawyer. The law must reflect a multi-faceted reality."

Conclusion

From the Other Side of the Screen
Ethel Baraona Pohl

A woman lives in a small town called Słubice. It is a border town in western Poland, closely linked to its German sister city Frankfurt (Oder), of which it was a part of until 1945. In this small town, as in the rest of the country, abortion is banned except in a few circumstances—sixty-nine percent of Poles view abortion as immoral and unacceptable. In this socio-cultural and political context, suddenly, a shadow overflies the sky. The woman looks up and has the feeling that something important is about to happen. The shadow starts getting darker as it comes closer, like an announcement of hope, and the sound gets louder from one second to the next. The shadow brings rain into a dry territory.

The woman is pregnant and wants to wield her abortion rights. But she can't, or rather could not. The shadow is a small drone that is bringing abortion pills from a country where abortion is legal, and delivering it to this border town where abortion is severely restricted.

Before it was only a shadow, then it was a drone. Now, it is an angel.

The image of the drone has been absorbed by our collective imaginary in so many ways, provoking everything from deep feelings of dread to the highest hopes of freedom. Important debates are currently taking place about military policies, political implications, and economies of the drone industry; nevertheless, and similarly important, are considerations about the social,

UNMANNED ARCHITECTURE AND SECURITY SERIES

Illustration of the book 'Atlas Marianus' by
Wilhelm Gumppenberg (Jaecklin, 1659)

psychological and emotional impact of living surrounded by the immanent presence of drones.

In Western countries—particularly those that have declared "war on terror"—and from the other side of the screen, it is difficult to know if a drone is documenting an event, filming a music video, monitoring weather, taking panoramic photos or bringing abortion pills into conservative countries. The myriad ways in which they can be used, from militarized killing machines to beneficial devices observing disaster situations, opens a debate that stretches wider than politics and economics to tackle humanitarian, social and ethical concerns. These, usually dismissed by politicians and policy-makers, are important because they deal with the intangible—traditions and context-based cultural interpretations.

The drone theme can be easily paired with science fiction and other new narratives, where a vehicle capable of flying without a pilot captures our imagination by the random beauty of the possibilities behind this idea. Sadly, we're talking about the beauty of fear. Immanence—*the divine presence*—can be the word that better describes the feeling and thoughts that materialize when one hears the word "drone." From the constant shadow over countries with targeted individuals, to the unstoppable Twitter feed that emerges when you search the hashtag #drone, the murmur of the drone's presence in the sky resonates from miles away. Inner fear deriving from its presence can be defined as a transcendent experience—an experience beyond the normal or physical level—provoked by an element that is always there, even if you're not able to see it. Is not a coincidence that the laser-targeting marker used to direct hellfire from a drone is called "the light of God" by marines and the military, according to video artist Omer Fast in his film *Five Thousand Feet is the Best*. Fast explains:

> "… the Marines like to call it the Light of God. It's a laser-targeting marker. We just send out a beam of laser and when the troops put on their night vision goggles they'll

just see this light that looks like it's coming from heaven. Right on the spot, coming out of nowhere, from the sky. It's quite beautiful."

The delusion of the omniscience of the drone subsequently causes the delusion of omnipotence, the fiction that a drone possesses unlimited power. In fact, all these feelings provoked by the constant shadow of the drone can be linked with otherworldly—even religious—traditions; feelings that are intertwined with concepts such as immanence, omniscience, transcendence and omnipotence. In this scenario, "you can run but you can't hide" is a popular motto commonly used when referring to drone strikes, which entails a strong truth about the impossibility of hiding away not only in physical terms, but also in spiritual, emotional and psychological ones. This impossibility of hiding can be related to the Christian feeling of fear after committing a sin: you can hide from everybody but not from the eyes of god; as a Predator drone operator wrote in his memoirs: "…sometimes I felt like God hurling thunderbolts from afar."[1] But references stream not only from Christianity; mythological allusions can also be found in this context. One of the latest improvements in drone technologies is called Autonomous Real-Time Ground Ubiquitous Surveillance Imaging System (ARGUS-IS), alluding in its acronym to the Greek mythological figure of Argos Panoptes—a giant with one hundred eyes[2]—since it fuses together data from three hundred and sixty-eight cellphone cameras to create a composite image of 1.8 billion pixels. Drones are the creation of power structures, and what power structure is stronger than our own beliefs?

The drone phenomena should be understood as part of a wider ecosystem, which has two main bodies, one physical and the other intangible. The physical body is formed by species of devices: the drones themselves; the network that makes possible the connections between the drone and the pilot, even if they are thousand of miles away; the network's vast infrastructure, in the form of data centers, internet connections and so on; and the physical places where the pilots spend their time controlling the distant targets. On the other side of the spectrum, the drone inhabits an intangible, seamless ecosystem formed by a set of emotional and psychological layers such as solitude, fear, loneliness, disbelief and ethical concerns. We can say, then, that we are all species belonging to this large infrastructure if we define it as "bare life," referring to Giorgio Agamben's notion of life reduced to its natural, biological dimension and excluded from the political community.[3]

As such, all our ideas about drones are basically illusory. We'll never know if author Richard Brautigan was predicting unmanned aerial vehicles when he wrote *All Watched Over by Machines of Loving Grace*; but it seems possible, since if we listen to conversations about drones, people tend to endow them with a soul. References to drone activities, military or not, abundantly use expressions such as "the drone can see enemies, target them…" This obscure humanization of the drone gives an ontological dimension to the debate. In that sense, the relationship between humans and machines goes far beyond the traditional; we need to reconsider our understanding of the human, and his role as a drone pilot, insofar as drones operate on a threshold in which life is both inside and outside the "killing machine."

All these considerations reveal that we are somehow living in a post-utopian world, particularly when reflecting on the architectural and spatial manifestations of utopias, which have been commonly envisioned to overcome the aerial space, a formerly wide and open field for design experimentation. Today, it seems that the space for utopias has been conquered to become a battlefield; fantasy and fear vis-à-vis. "The sky here is not merely a space for flight. It is a space for the transmission and reception of command, control, communications, computation, and intelligence," as Honor Harger wrote.[4] Our fantasies are made of dreams, but what happens when there's no more space for dreams? Constant dreamed of a *New Babylon* occupying the space above the ground with a pattern that can grow progressively, an open framework ready to cover all the surface of Earth; and by doing so, he transformed our notions of the politics of the atmosphere.[5] Following similar formal principles, Yona Friedman developed his concept of *Ville spatiale*–the Spatial City–in the early 1960s. As in the *New Babylon*, *La Ville Spatiale* is raised on slender supports up above the earth; independent structures suspended over the old cities and the landscape. Moving upwards, above the first layer over ground, there is a whole set of avant garde projects intended to be built in the sky.

Already in 1726 in *Gulliver's Travels* Jonathan Swift described Laputa, an island city floating in the sky with an area of ten thousand acres. In the twentieth century, highly influenced by science fiction, several floating city projects materialized as speculative proposals. In the 1920s, Hugo Gernsback suggested that ten thousand years hence "a city the size of New York will float several miles above the surface of the earth, where the air is cleaner and purer and free from disease carrying bacteria."[6] In 1929, Georgii Krutikov designed his famous *Flying City*. More recently, and among many others, we have the 1966 *Urbland 2000* by François Dallegret. In these kinds of projects, the atmosphere suddenly becomes the basis for political action, as Mark Wigley has stated,[7] because it becomes a space for negotiation. As it is now.

How to understand and move through the dilemma of drones occupying a space for negotiation that is supposed to be a common space? We're not talking only about the negotiations on the use of the air space, but of a set of rules that navigate in the vast waters of the unspoken. Regulations on aerial space are becoming stricter on a daily basis, and all the hidden layers of policies dealing with this topic are not as transparent as they should, affecting the way we adapt to them. Can we ask ourselves if being visible from the sky is legally considered being in public? What happens on the other side of the screen—that can be thousand miles away from the visible drone—, in a space and time that is not visible at all? One of the biggest ironies of remote piloting is that aircrews have been removed from the dangers and humanity of their impact on the battlefield, while simultaneously attacks are increasing both in intensity and in territorial terms. The fear of the unknown becomes a way to govern and control.

However, this context can also be a perfect landscape to recover an utopian approach to airspace, transforming the battlefield in a space for dreams once again. Today, almost everyone can buy or build a drone, and all kind of uses have been envisioned for what was initially created as a weapon, from journalism to pizza-delivery drones. This is a natural reaction when a new technology is adopted for civic use, but after the hype and trendiness of "using-drones-for-everything," we must admit that are several fields of action where drones can be—and are indeed—helpful. In the past few months, researchers started using drones to look for corpses in hard-to-access locations,[8] or to monitorize the size of seabird colonies seeking to understand how climate change affects the Australian coastline. In both cases, scientists rave about how effective the use of drones has turned out to be.

"The modern civilian is, in a sense, as close to warfare as we have ever been," Henry Barnes recently wrote, pointing out how "through whistleblowers such as WikiLeaks, we have never been more aware of how our wars are being fought, even if the gaps in our knowledge are still huge."[9] We can add that this awareness allows us to understand and therefore to find the gap in the policies that sustain the uses of drones. There is an urgent need for a proper debate on the *politics of the atmosphere* again, and instead of accepting the weaponizing of airspace *in praise of security*, we should ask ourselves if we can reverse this approach and transform the silence and invisibility, from the other side of the screen, into a new political infrastructure based on an afterlife for the drone.

Beyond naiveté, this is not a conclusion, but an invitation to explore further the limits of what we know about drones, and turn this knowledge based on fantasy and fear into a new relationship between space and data. A drone transformed into a shadow, a shadow converted into a ghost, a ghost becoming real to inhabit the unknown. The unknown turned utopia.

UNMANNED ARCHITECTURE AND SECURITY SERIES

1. MJ Martin with CW Sasser. *Predator: The remote-control war over Iraq and Afghanistan; A pilot's story* (Zenith Press, 2010).
2. "Tech: ARGUS – The Great All Seeing Eye," *TechedOn*, January 28, 2013, accessed May 25, 2016, http://www.techedon.com/2013/01/28/technology/tech-argus-the-great-all-seeing-eye/
3. Giorgio Agamben. *Homo sacer: Sovereign power and bare life*, trans. D. Heller-Roazen (Stanford University Press, 1998).
4. Honor Harger, "Unmanned Aerial Ecologies: proto-drones, airspace and canaries in the mine," *honor harger*, April 21, 2013, accessed May 25, 2016, https://honorharger.wordpress.com/2013/04/21/unmanned-aerial-ecologies-proto-drones-airspace-and-canaries-in-the-mine/
5. Mark Wigley, *Constant's New Babylon. The Hyper-Architecture of Desire* (Witte de With, center of contemporary art / 010 Publishers, 1998).
6. Hugo Gernsback (ed.). *Air Wonder Stories* (Pulp Tales Press, 2013).
7. Wigley, *Constant's New Babylon*.
8. Tim Sandle, "Drones being used to scan for dead bodies", *Digital Journal*, April 29, 2016, accessed May 25, 2016, http://www.digitaljournal.com/news/odd+news/drones-being-used-to-scan-for-dead-bodies/article/464185
9. Henry Barnes, "Kill shots: why cinema has drone warfare in its sights", *The Guardian*, April 14, 2016, accessed May 25, 2016, https://www.theguardian.com/film/2016/apr/14/eye-in-the-sky-london-has-fallen-drone-films

Contributors

Ethel Baraona Pohl is Critic, writer and curator. Co-founder with César Reyes of the independent research studio and publishing house dpr-barcelona, which operates in the fields of architecture, political theory and the social milieu. Editor of *Quaderns d'arquitectura i urbanisme* from 2011-2016, and contributor to several magazines and books. Her writing appears in *Open Source Architecture* (Thames and Hudson, 2015), *The Form of Form* (Lars Muller, 2016), *Together! The New Architecture of the Collective* (Ruby Press, 2017), *Architecture is All Over* (Columbia Books of Architecture, 2017), *Inéditos 2017* (La Casa Encendida, 2017), *Harvard Design Magazine*, and *Volume*, among others. Curator of the third Think Space program with the theme "Money'"; also curator (together with César Reyes and Pelin Tan) of the exhibition "Adhocracy ATHENS" at the Onassis Cultural Centre, 2015, winner of the ADI Culture Award 2016. Director of Foros 2017, the architecture lecture series of the UIC Barcelona School of Architecture. Since 2016, dpr-barcelona is platform member of Future Architecture, the first pan-European platform of architecture museums, festivals and producers.

Josh Begley is a data artist and web developer based in Brooklyn. His work has appeared in *New York Magazine*, *The New York Times*, NPR, *The Atlantic*, and at the New Museum of Contemporary Art. Appropriating publicly available satellite imagery, Begley's work takes advantage of application programing interfaces, or APIs, to build collections of machine-generated images about quotidian life. In 2012, Begley created Drones+, an iPhone app designed to send users a notice every time a drone strike is reported in the news. Now known as Metadata+, it was rejected from the App Store five times due to "excessively objectionable or crude content," before being accepted by Apple in 2014. Begley holds degrees from the University of California, Berkeley and New York University. He currently works at *The Intercept*, a publication of First Look Media.

The Center for the Study of the Drone is an interdisciplinary research and education project at Bard College. The Center studies autonomous and semi-autonomous systems, which it sees as one of the most significant technological developments of our time—not only because of its implications for warfare, but also

CONTRIBUTORS

for its civilian applications and its potential to influence our relationship with our physical environment and each other. The Center sponsors research, art, education and dialogue in order to promote drone literacy, inquiry and, ultimately, to contribute to the development of sensible policies to govern drone use, both in times of war and peace, by government, enterprise and civilians alike. The Center develops free written and multimedia content, designs open-source curricula, sponsors original research and maintains a schedule of public lectures and panel discussions. By bringing together practitioners from disparate fields such as Computer Science, the Arts, Literature, International Relations, Human Rights, History and Media Studies, the Center seeks to engender a diverse and dynamic public conversation. The Center for the Study of the Drone was founded in 2012 by two undergraduates, Arthur Holland Michel and Dan Gettinger, and a group of faculty including Thomas Keenan, Roger Berkowitz, Keith O'Hara and Maria Cecire.

Quirine Eijkman is a Senior Researcher and Lecturer at the Centre for Terrorism and Counterterrorism, Leiden University. Additionally, she is a consultant for Justice Q&A. Previously she worked for the Police and Human Rights Program of Amnesty International, the Human Rights Committee of the Dutch Advisory Council on International Affairs, the Roosevelt Academy of Utrecht University, the Netherlands Institute of Human Rights and at the International Humanitarian Law Department of the Netherlands Red Cross. Currently, she is a Member of the Board of UPEACE, the Hague, and a Member of the Board of Advisors of the Dutch Platform on Civil Rights and the Dutch Section of the International Commission of Jurists, where she was the Vice-President between 2005 and 2011. She has published on the side effects of security measures for human rights, police reform, and human rights mobilization. Her areas of interest include security and human rights, counter-terrorism, transitional justice and the sociology of law.

Dan Gettinger is an American photographer, researcher and writer. He is the co-director of the Center for the Study of the Drone at Bard College. Dan's interests are in military history, technology and strategy.

Arthur Holland Michel is a Peruvian-born, quad-continental researcher, editor and writer based in Brooklyn, New York. He is the co-director of the Center for the Study of the Drone at Bard College, an interdisciplinary research and education project, which he founded with Dan Gettinger and a group of faculty in 2012.

Catherine Harwood is a PhD candidate at the Grotius Centre for International Legal Studies at Leiden University. Her research explores how international fact-finding investigations in post-conflict situations may be coordinated and harmonized to strengthen international justice and accountability. Harwood graduated cum laude from Leiden University in 2012 with a Masters of Law in Advanced Studies of Public

International Law, with the assistance of a Rotary Vocational Scholarship. Harwood worked for two years as a Judges Clerk at the New Zealand Court of Appeal and was a teaching fellow and researcher at Victoria University. She has also interned at the International Criminal Court and the International Bar Association's Program on the ICC.

Yael Messer is an independent curator. She has participated in the De Appel Curatorial Program, Amsterdam. Messer has collaborated internationally with museums, institutions and independent art spaces. She is the recipient of the 2013 Artist grant for her curatorial collaboration with the 13th Istanbul Biennial.

Lieutenant-colonel Pieter Mink is the senior advisor UAS at the Army Staff at Utrecht. In this position he is also responsible for flight safety, quality and airworthiness of UAS. Lt.Col Pieter Mink served in three missions. UNPROFOR as a UN Military Observer in Bosnia from July 1993—February 1994. In the SFIR mission, from July 2004—March 2005, he served in the MN Division CS at Al Hillah, Iraq. In this division he was as staff officer G7 responsible for all training of the Iraqi National Guard. During his final mission from July 2009—February 2010 he served in HQ ISAF, Kabul, as a planning staff officer Information Operations.

Marina Otero Verzier is an architect based in Rotterdam. She is Director of Research at Het Nieuwe Instituut, and the Curator of WORK, BODY, LEISURE, the Dutch Pavilion at the 16th Venice International Architecture Biennale in 2018. With the After Belonging Agency, Otero was Chief Curator of the Oslo Architecture Triennale 2016, which addressed the implications of architecture in contemporary processes of displacement and identity construction. From 2011-2015 Otero was based in New York. In 2014, as Director of Global Network Programming at Studio-X (Columbia University's GSAPP), she launched the research series on 'Security Regimes,' examining global spaces of exception. Her work, recently awarded by The Graham Foundation, Design Trust, and the FAD Thought and Criticism Award, has been published in different books and journals. Otero has co-edited *Promiscuous Encounters* (2014), *Unmanned: Architecture and Security Series* (2016), *After Belonging: The Objects, Spaces, and Territories of the Ways We Stay In Transit* (2016). She currently teaches the seminar "Political practices in architecture: borders, bodies, spaces" at ETSA Madrid and the architectural design studio "Domestic Institutions" at the Royal College of Art in London. Otero studied architecture at TU Delft and ETSA Madrid. In 2013, as a Fulbright Scholar, she graduated from the M.S. in Critical, Curatorial and Conceptual Practices in Architecture at Columbia University GSAPP. She completed her PhD at ETSAM in 2016.

Ruben Pater is an Amsterdam-based Dutch designer. He has as a mission to create visual narratives about complex political issues. His *Drone Survival Guide* received wide attention in 2013 as an educational tool on drones, functioning as a

CONTRIBUTORS

political statement. Pater's other projects include *The First Dutch Flood Manual*, a research into disaster communication in times of climate change, and *Double Standards*, a research about maritime trade and Somali piracy. Pater currently teaches at the communication department of the Design Academy in Eindhoven and is working on a citizen journalism project in countries with censorship.

Bradley Samuels is a founding partner at SITU Research, a practice focused on developing and implementing new strategies for visualizing, mapping, modeling, and analyzing human rights violations for legal and advocacy contexts. SITU recently launched the Spatial Practice as Evidence and Advocacy (SPEA) project. SPEA casework, undertaken in collaboration with a diverse range human rights organizations, news outlets, legal counsel, scientists and researchers, focuses on the collection and synthesis of disparate forms of spatial evidence, both quantitative and qualitative, that may be gathered in a specific case such as satellite imagery, video footage, digital and parametric modeling, the verbatim testimony of witnesses and munitions specifications, among others. SITU Research has worked with Human Rights Watch, B'tselem, FIDH, the United Nations Special Rapporteur on counter terrorism and human rights, Forensic Architecture and attorney Michael Sfard, among others, and has received grants from the MacArthur Foundation, the Oak Foundation, the European Research Council, the National Science Foundation and the New York State Council for the Arts. Samuels teaches in the studio sequence in the undergraduate Barnard / Columbia Architecture program, and has lectured widely on the intersection of design, technology, and human rights. Samuels holds a BA from Vassar College in Art History and a BArch from the Cooper Union School of Architecture. SITU Research is a division of SITU—a parent organization that also is home to the design practice SITU Studio and the digital fabrication practice SITU Fabrication.

Naureen Shah is a legislative counsel at the ACLU's Washington legislative office. She advocates for U.S. government practices that respect and uphold human rights, with a current focus on abusive law enforcement practices impacting American Muslim communities. She is a frequent commentator on U.S. human rights practices and national security policies. Her articles include "Drones: From Bad Habit to Terrible Policy" (Reuters, Jan. 2014); "Kindle for the Drone Debate" (*Roll Call*, Jan. 2014); "Times for the Truth about 'Targeted Killings'" (*The Guardian*, Oct. 22, 2013); "The FBI's Surveillance Power in the aftermath of Boston" (*The Hill*, May 17, 2013); and "End Covert Drone War" (*USA Today*, Feb. 7, 2013), among others. Shah is the co-author of "Illusion of Justice: Human Rights Abuses in U.S. Terrorism Prosecutions" by Human Rights Watch and the Columbia Law School Human Rights Institute, and co-author of major reports on drone strikes: *The Civilian Impact of Drones, Counting Drone Strike Deaths* and *Targeting With Drone Technology: Humanitarian Law Implications*.

Malkit Shoshan is the founder and director of the architectural think tank FAST: Foundation for Achieving Seamless Territory. FAST uses research, advocacy, and design to investigate the relationship between architecture, urban planning, and human rights in conflict and post-conflict areas. Shoshan is the author and the map maker of the award-winning book *Atlas of Conflict: Israel-Palestine* (Uitgeverij 010, 2010) and the co-author of the book *Village. One Land Two Systems and Platform Paradise* (Damiani Editore, 2014). Additional publications include Zoo, or the letter Z, just after zionism (NAiM, 2012), the issue Spaces of Conflict. *Footprint*, TU Delft Architecture Theory Journal (JAP SAM Books, 2017) and *BLUE: Peacekeeping Architecture* (Actar, 2018). In 2016, Shoshan was the curator of the Dutch Pavilion for The Venice Architecture Biennale with the exhibition BLUE: Architecture of UN Peacekeeping Missions. She is currently an international scholar at the Institute for Public Knowledge at NYU and a Ph.D. fellow at the Delft University of Technology. In 2015, she was a visiting critic at Syracuse University's School of Architecture and in 2016, she taught a course Architecture of Peace at the Harvard Graduate School of Design. Shoshan was a finalist for the Harvard GSD's Wheelwright Prize in 2014.

Matthew Stadler is a writer. He has written five novels and received several awards and fellowships in recognition of his work. More recently, he wrote the book *Deventer*, a story about hope and power in architecture. In addition, Stadler gave last year's Premsela lecture, in which he speculated on the role of drone technologies in a surveillance state, among many other things. A Dutch translation of this text, "Interior Decorating in War-Time," was recently published in *De Gids*.

Liam Young is an architect who operates in the spaces between design, fiction and futures. He is founder of the urban futures think tank Tomorrow's Thoughts Today (TTT), a group whose work explores the possibilities of fantastic, perverse and imaginary urbanisms. With TTT he has consulted and conducted workshops on speculation, emerging technologies and future forecasting for firms including Arup—Drivers for Change, Phillips Technologies, BBC, the film industry and various arts and science organizations. His projects include *Under Tomorrows Sky*, a science fiction movie set for a fictional future city developed through collaborations with scientists and technologists, and *Electronic Countermeasures*, a swarm of quad copter drones that drift through the city broadcasting a pirate internet and file sharing hub.

Eyal Weizman is an architect, Professor of Visual Cultures and director of the Centre for Research Architecture at Goldsmiths, University of London. Since 2011 he is also Director of the European Research Council funded project, Forensic Architecture, on the place of architecture in international humanitarian law. Since 2007 he has been a founding member of the architectural collective DAAR in Beit Sahour/Palestine.

Drone. Unmanned
Architecture and Security Series

Editors Ethel Baraona Pohl, Marina Otero Verzier, Malkit Shoshan

Contributors Josh Begley, Dan Gettinger, Catherine Harwood, Arthur Holland Mitchel, Yael Messer, Ruben Pater, Francesca Recchia, Gilad Reich, Bradley Samuels Naureen Shah, Matthew Stadler, Jane Szita

Editorial Assistance Vera Sacchetti

Copyediting Jess Ngan, Vera Sacchetti

Design Numa Merino Studio

ISBN 978-84-944873-4-7
Legal deposit B 6345-2018

Publisher dpr-barcelona

This book is set in Dutch 801 and Swiss 721. It is printed on Munken Cream 80g paper, generated with Print on Demand Technology

Printed edition first published in February 2018

dpr-barcelona
Viladomat 59 4o 4a
08015 Barcelona

w dpr-barcelona.com
tw @dpr_barcelona

This book is licensed under a Creative Commons Attribution–NonCommercial–NoDerivatives 4.0 License. It allows sharing but not commercial nor derivative use of the material in any medium or format.

This publication was made possible through the generous support of the Graham Foundation for Advanced Studies in the Fine Arts, the Het Nieuwe Instituut, and the Creative Industries Fund NL.

Graham Foundation

Het Nieuwe Instituut

architectuur
design
e-cultuur

creative industries fund NL

Every effort has been made to trace copyright holders and to obtain their permission for the use of copyright material. In the event of any copyright holder being inadvertently omitted, please contact the publishers directly. Any corrections should be incorporated in future reprints or editions of this book.